PORTFOLIO

PORTFOLIO

KILLER CUSTOMERS

Larry Selden is a professor emeritus of finance and economics at Columbia University Graduate School of Business, a prominent consultant, and an adviser to senior executives in many industries.

Geoffrey Colvin, *Fortune* magazine's senior editor at large, is coanchor of *Wall Street Week with Fortune* on PBS, the most widely viewed business program on Amercian television.

Killer Customers

Tell the Good from the Bad—
and Crush Your Competitors

Larry Selden
&
Geoffrey Colvin

Previously published as
Angel Customers & Demon Customers

PORTFOLIO

PORTFOLIO
Published by the Penguin Group
Penguin Group (USA) Inc., 375 Hudson Street,
New York, New York 10014, U.S.A.
Penguin Group (Canada), 10 Alcorn Avenue,
Toronto, Ontario, Canada M4V 3B2 (a division of Pearson Penguin Canada Inc.)
Penguin Books Ltd, 80 Strand, London WC2R 0RL, England
Penguin Ireland, 25 St Stephen's Green, Dublin 2, Ireland (a division of Penguin Books Ltd)
Penguin Group (Australia), 250 Camberwell Road, Camberwell,
Victoria 3124, Australia (a division of Pearson Australia Group Pty Ltd)
Penguin Books India Pvt Ltd, 11 Community Centre, Panchsheel Park, New Delhi - 110 017, India
Penguin Books (NZ), cnr Airborne and Rosedale Roads, Albany,
Auckland, New Zealand (a division of Pearson New Zealand Ltd)
Penguin Books (South Africa) (Pty) Ltd, 24 Sturdee Avenue,
Rosebank, Johannesburg 2196, South Africa

Penguin Books Ltd, Registered Offices:
80 Strand, London WC2R 0RL, England

First published in the United States of America as *Angel Customers & Demon Customers: Discover Which Is Which
and Turbo-Charge Your Stock* by Portfolio, a member of Penguin Group (USA) Inc. 2003
This paperback edition published 2004

1 3 5 7 9 10 8 6 4 2

PUBLISHER'S NOTE
This publication is designed to provide accurate and authoritative information in regard to the subject matter
covered. It is sold with the understanding that the publisher is not engaged in rendering legal, accounting or
other professional services. If you require legal advice or other expert assistance, you should seek the services of
a competent professional.

CIP data available.
ISBN 1-59184-007-4 (hc.)
ISBN 1-59184-042-2 (pbk.)

Printed in the United States of America
Set in AGaramond
Designed by Erin Benach

To my parents, Marguerite and Nathan, for teaching me the joy of learning.—L.S.

To my parents, for lifelong unwavering encouragement.—G.C.

Acknowledgments

I want to thank my wife, Yoko, for her continual encouragement in writing this book. I had always been afraid of how much work such an endeavor might be, and thanks to her impetus I found it was far more demanding than I had feared. She suggested the very important Customer Value Exchange Model as a way to integrate the key elements of the book—the customer perspective, and the shareowner perspective. We are also indebted to her tireless efforts in reading and rereading numerous drafts, making innumerable improvements at every stage. Her love and support are a continual source of energy. Having worked with me in applying many of these concepts in companies all over the world, she has been my toughest critic and staunchest ally. Many thanks to Alex, my son, for offering valuable insights along the way.

Geoff and I also want to thank my students at Columbia University over the past few years for providing a laboratory in which to test some of these ideas at a time when the concepts were in their crudest forms.

—L.S.

I owe deepest thanks to my colleagues at *Fortune* and the rest of Time Inc., particularly Rik Kirkland and John Huey for not trying to talk me out of this project as it consumed growing portions of my time, and to them and Joe Nocera, Ned Desmond, and Jim Aley for publishing early versions of this work in *Fortune* and *Business 2.0*.

Larry and I both wish to thank our publisher, Adrian Zackheim, for sticking with us as this book evolved into something markedly different from the project we first proposed to him. His enthusiasm and confidence sustained us. We owe thanks also to Bob Barnett of Williams & Connolly, whose expertise in representing us was simply invaluable.

I must thank most especially my own angels, my wife and sons, whose patience through the overwhelming demands of book writing and whose understanding in the face of countless blown personal deadlines went far beyond what I could ever have expected or deserved.

—G.C.

Contents

Foreword

The principles of the first edition of this book were based on years of observations and experience with companies struggling to put the customer at the center of their business. Since hardcover publication, we have tested those principles much further through our work with many companies in widely different industries. In addition, we have delivered lectures to thousands of managers and investors on the huge shareowner value potential of managing companies as portfolios of customers, and they've told us about their own lessons learned. These experiences only reinforce our belief that in the face of endless management fads that come and go, putting customers truly at the center of your business is an enduring competitive advantage. Everything else, emphatically including such recent managerial fashions as outsourcing and growth-motivated acquisitions, pales in comparison to the competitive power of getting the customer experience right.

As ever more managers, consultants, and academics bandy about the term "customer-centricity," we find that senior managers increasingly struggle with defining it. Sounds great, but just what is it? Customer-centricity is *winning with customers*. The "with" is critical. A company is customer-centric if and only if it delivers a thrilling total experience to the customer *and* in exchange is rewarded with exceptional levels of profitability. This is the key notion of a Mutually Beneficial Value Exchange discussed in Chapter 7. If a company is profitable but delivers an inferior value proposition, it's only a matter of time before competitors steal its customers and associated profit opportunity. If a company delivers dominant customer experiences but can't make a buck at it, investors will sooner or later pull the funding plug. But if the value exchange is mutually beneficial, the company can and should reinvest a significant portion of its profits in creating new and better value propositions for existing and new customers.

Readers tell us one of the most striking and powerful assertions in this book is our statement that a company's top 20 percent of customers by profitability typically generate more than 120 percent of the company's profits, while the bottom 20 percent of customers typically generate losses equaling more than 100 percent of profits. Our experience since publication has reinforced this observation time and again.

When first confronted with this assertion, virtually all CEOs tell us we're crazy—*their* company is different, they insist. Inevitably they are astonished and intrigued when we confirm our hypothesized profitability distribution in their companies after we teach their own employees how to do the analysis. Then the questions start flying: Who are these customers? Why does their profitability vary so widely? Where are the opportunities for us, and how can we seize them? Probably for the first time, a real appetite develops at the CEO level to segment customers into groups with homogeneous needs, so they can be approached, acquired, and insulated from competitive attack.

Companies find support for customer-centricity everywhere. Every sales organization wants to thrill customers, and putting customers at the center gives them a chance to do what they love. Employees naturally want to thrill customers, if only the corporate bureaucracy would get out of the way. Investors are wide open to a customer-centric story on why to buy the stock. A $50 share price could easily be $100 once investors understand how a company can grow its most profitable customer segments or can fix, close, or sell its least profitable segments. These are billion-dollar opportunities. All our real-world experience and learning since this book's first publication has reinforced the shareowner potential of the customer.

Because the top 20 percent and bottom 20 percent of customers are so central to any company's success or failure, we've chosen to title this edition *Killer Customers*. Winning with the top 20 percent on a sustained basis will kill your competitors; not dealing with the bottom 20 percent will kill you. In the earlier edition we called the top customers Angels. The bottom 20 percent is a bit more complicated. Some are unprofitable because your company can't figure out a way to serve them profitably. Others—typically just a few—are unprofitable because they exhibit abusive customer behavior, seeking ways to cheat your company, for example by making excessive returns, tying up staff for incredibly long periods, or occasionally outright deception. This latter group we refer to as Demons. To win, every company must deal successfully with both types of its Killer Customers.

Nothing we've learned diminishes our belief that cultural and political obstacles are the most threatening barriers to success. Only the CEO has the clout to cut through the negative, evil forces that are focused on preserving bureaucratic power at all costs and that obstruct the learning necessary for moving from a product- or service- or function-centric company to a customer-centric one. Every employee is watching the CEO's commitment and worrying about whether this is yet another initiative or the *strategy*. Like anything of significant, lasting value, creating a truly customer-centric company is tough. One of the CEO's most important roles is to mandate customer centricity as the *strategy*—avoiding the pitfall of making it just one of many projects or initiatives.

In this book we've portrayed Royal Bank of Canada as a star. It continues to excel and has taken its game to even higher levels on two fronts.

First, in early 2003 Vice Chairman Jim Rager and his leadership of RBC's Canadian retail bank began diligently applying the customer segmentation principles outlined in Chapter 6 to drill down on their existing segments and search out highly attractive subsegments. Working through a series of workshops, key segment teams identified critical subsegments of customers that shared very precise common needs. Certain of these subsegments were key to RBC's current exceptional level of profitability. Others represented exceptional new profit growth opportunities. To meet the common needs of each subsegment, the teams further developed new or refined Value Propositions. For each subsegment, RBC applied its world-class customer profitability models to assess the current level of profitability and then to estimate the incremental revenue and profit potential of each candidate Value Proposition.

One of the new customer subsegments, called Snowbirds, has already begun being served quite successfully with new Value Propositions. As the Wealth Preserver customer segment team began to probe its population of Canadian customers, examining their behavior, they uncovered an interesting insight. A significant portion of the most profitable Wealth Preservers spends a good portion of the winter in Florida and Arizona.

As the team studied this newly identified subsegment's behavior and needs, they discovered a huge new business opportunity. These customers were encountering many difficulties trying to bank in a foreign country. They wanted to borrow money to buy winter homes, establish credit, and easily change Canadian dollars into U.S. currency. Overarching all of this was that they missed the great service they'd been accustomed to with RBC in Canada. French-speaking Canadians encountered special problems. U.S. banks didn't understand these customers and weren't equipped to meet their needs.

In responding to this opportunity, RBC had a secret weapon: the newly opened branches of its U.S. subsidiary, RBC Centura. The management of RBC Centura hadn't focused on serving the customers of its parent when they were in the U.S. The Snowbird subsegment represented a unique opportunity on which to collaborate. Very quickly, new Value Propositions for Snowbirds were developed and tested along the lines discussed in Chapter 7. By mid-March 2004, the results were exceptional, and scaling was well underway. The opportunity of almost 800,000 potential Snowbirds in Florida, more than half of whom own property there, had been addressed with amazing speed and focus. This speaks volumes about the power of really putting customers at the center.

The second way RBC has taken its game to a higher level is by becoming a leader in communicating its customer-centricity work to investors. Late in 2003, RBC banking reported publicly its profitability by customer deciles (i.e., it ranked its roughly 11 million individual customers based on profitability from best to worst and then grouped then into ten clusters of about 1.1 million each). Even more impressive and insightful for investors, RBC also disclosed those deciles within each of its three high-level customer segments. The bank showed how the profitability distribution improved over time, with profitability improving for each decile and segment. We're not aware of any other financial institution, or in fact any other company on the planet, that has provided such customer-centric disclosure. With regard to its new Value Proposition work, the news is decidedly good: RBC reported in January that it is on schedule to achieve the $100-million revenue increase targeted for 2004.

Best Buy, a company we refer to only fleetingly in the text, began the journey toward true customer-centricity early in 2003, as we were finishing the book's manuscript. At that time Best Buy was widely viewed as the class act in consumer electronics but was being challenged by two formidable non-traditional competitors, Wal-Mart and Dell. These heavyweights were starting to move into consumer electronics.

At about the same time, Best Buy CEO Brad Anderson and his leadership were first exposed to the principles of *Angel Customers and Demon Customers* and were challenged on why Best Buy's P/E ratio, which had for a number of years stood at a premium to the S&P 500, had slipped to below average—despite Best Buy earning one of the highest rates of profitability in retail. The market seemed to be signaling that the prospect of Wal-Mart and Dell moving into consumer electronics could threaten Best Buy's ability to continue to earn superior profitability. Best Buy needed a new basis for differentiation in the changing competitive landscape.

Anderson and his top team were shown data compiled over an astonishingly few months demonstrating the typical high concentration of profitable and unprofitable customers. Armed with this insight, together with data about who those customers were and why they were profitable or unprofitable, Anderson and his team began to follow the road map outlined in our book. Thousands of copies of the book were distributed in headquarters and to store managers and employees. The leaders identified key customer segments, some of whom drove current profitability and others that represented huge new profitable growth opportunities.

Best Buy continued to work intensely through the spring, developing initial Value Propositions for the targeted customer segments. A set of four lab stores were selected in the Washington, D.C., area to test the delivery of these Value Propositions on real customers. Could Mutually Beneficial Value Exchanges be created in which Best Buy's customers would receive unique and highly valued experiences and Best Buy would earn exceptional levels of profitability? Building on the encouraging learnings, another 28 stores were introduced into the lab program through the summer and early fall.

Beginning in the winter, Wall Street began to understand that something big might be brewing at Best Buy and began writing about the new customer-centric model. Most encouragingly, the stock started to recover some of its prior gloss. In fact, in January 2004, *Forbes* named Best Buy the best managed company in America. Like RBC, Best Buy is on a journey to reinvent itself from a position of industry leadership and outstanding financial performance.

Many other companies in a wide range of industries are making the journey toward genuine customer-centricity, using the principles we've described. A major corporate bank, a major hospitality chain, and a major information technology company are all in the midst of this journey as we write. As we speak about these ideas to business audiences across the country—audiences from 10 to 2,000—we're continually struck by how managers in every industry immediately grasp the significance of what we're saying, and how it can make their own companies more valuable.

Most of all, we're heartened to see managers understand and then prove to us through their own actions and their own results that true customer-centricity is an awesome competitive advantage. That's why we believe even more strongly now than we did at the time of the first edition that the competitive order in most industries will be determined in large part by which players commit themselves to these principles, and when.

The revolution is underway, and you have no time to lose.

We wish you the very best of success.

Larry Selden and Geoffrey Colvin
2004

Killer Customers

△ 1 ▽

The Trillion-Dollar Opportunity You're Missing

What It Means—and What
It's Worth—to Be Truly
Customer Centered

True Story

A customer of a major money-center bank wanted a mortgage recently. He looked like every bank's dream customer. He's a highly active trader through the bank's stock brokerage services, paying huge commissions, which are extremely profitable for the bank. He also keeps lots of money in the bank, and those large balances are very profitable as well. One thing he didn't do was borrow much from the bank—his current mortgage was with another institution. Note: Mortgages can be *highly* profitable for banks. So when the day came that this customer wanted to refinance his old mortgage, he called the bank's mortgage department. He was sure they'd be delighted to hear from such a terrific customer as him.

It was as if he had called the Bank of Outer Mongolia.

The mortgage department had no idea whether he was a good customer or a bad one—highly profitable or break-even or unprofitable.

They gave him the same treatment and made him the same offer as if he were a stranger who had walked in off the street. He would have to fill out endless paperwork, even though the bank already had much of it. He would have to pay the same fees and interest rates as anyone else. When would the bank make a firm offer of the terms of the mortgage? They couldn't really say. In fact, the mortgage department—being ignorant of the customer's history with the bank—couldn't even offer him assurances that he'd get the mortgage at all.

Instead of just being miffed, this customer called the manager of the branch where he has his account—a manager who knew just how valuable this guy was. Then he patched in a manager from the bank's mortgage department. These two managers had never spoken to each other before. Didn't it make sense, asked the customer, for him to get his mortgage and get it at advantageous rates in light of his long history and high profitability with the bank? If he didn't, he'd certainly see if some other bank could be more accommodating.

"Sorry," said the mortgage manager, who explained that his hands were tied. This bank, like most major banks today, is the product of several mergers, and after the last big one all mortgage managers were put on a very short leash until the integration got worked through. He was strictly forbidden to do anything special for this or any other customer.

"Wait!," said the branch manager, now pleading with the mortgage manager in an effort to keep this customer. "I'll pay you the first-year costs of giving this customer a better mortgage deal—just give it to him! Make him happy! We make loads of money with this guy!" "Sorry," said the mortgage manager. "I'm not allowed."

The customer got his mortgage someplace else, at an institution that could see what he was worth and was hungry for the business. He gradually began shifting his trading from the Bank of Outer Mongolia to the new institution as well. So the bank not only blew a great opportunity to deepen its relationship with this highly profitable customer, it let a direct competitor take a significant piece of the customer's business. And it made the customer angry—a lose-lose deal. Bottom line: a complete disaster for the bank. It's no surprise to find that this bank's financial performance is lousy. Its ROE (return on equity)[1] is a dismal 10 percent and falling; profits and its stock price have been plunging, and its P/E (price-earnings) multiple is much worse than mediocre, about half the average P/E for the S&P 500. As we write this, the newspapers are full of rumors that the CEO's days are numbered.

Sound like any bank you've done business with?

Now suppose that instead of this ludicrous, frustrating experience, the customer had encountered something different. Suppose the manager he spoke to wasn't in charge of mortgages or a branch but was in charge of him and customers like him. The manager knew everything about the customer's relationship with every part of the bank and exactly how profitable he was because this information was available on a computer screen at any time. More important, this manager was *accountable* for the profitability of this customer and others like him. A few layers up in the organization was an executive whose entire job was to manage the customer segment to which this customer belonged (the bank might call the segment something like "wealth builders"). Other parts of the bank—mortgages, deposit accounts, brokerage services, branches—functioned as internal suppliers of products, services, and distribution to this executive and the handful of other executives who were in charge of other customer segments.

Does this sound crazy? Let's get really radical: Suppose these segment executives had profit-and-loss responsibility. Suppose the bank could calculate the profitability of each individual customer or customer segment, and these executives were on the hook to deliver specific, budgeted improvements in their segment's profit each quarter.

In this kind of organization, what kind of experience would our bank customer have had? Most likely one that was markedly better—for him and for the bank.

This fantasy bank is no fantasy. It's Toronto–based Royal Bank, which has reorganized its huge Personal and Commercial division in exactly this way. The results have been astonishing. The division has reduced expenses by $1 billion, in part because those product areas— mortgages, deposit accounts, etc.—are no longer fiefdoms with their own separate administrative infrastructures and their own marketing efforts, which were often aimed in an uncoordinated way at the same customers; everyone in the bank realized that loads of money was being wasted as a result, yet it was virtually impossible to do anything about it. At the same time, the division is ahead of schedule in increasing revenues by $1 billion, a natural result of trying to meet customers' total needs rather than trying to sell individual products and services. That's a *$2 billion swing*, which the bank is sure resulted from its new approach to business. Because of the bank's high fixed-cost structure, most of that money fell to the bottom line. By contrast with the financial performance of the Bank of Outer Mongolia, Royal Bank's Personal and Commercial division earns a return on equity of about 25 percent. If the division was a freestanding business, we calculate that its excellent profitability and growth prospects would win it a P/E greater than the S&P 500 average—even though most banks' P/E multiples are way below the average. And the stock of the corporation has outperformed that of most North American financial institutions over the period.

Other than these radically different financial results, what's the difference between Royal Bank and the bank that failed so dismally in dealing with our unhappy customer? Not much, by most criteria. They're both giant, long-established banks offering a full line of financial services to millions of customers. Both have computers loaded with stunning amounts of potentially useful data about those customers. The most important difference between them is much deeper than matters of size, products, or even the business they're in. It is that these banks conceive of the way they do business in profoundly different ways. Specifically, one of them, Royal Bank, has put *customers at the center.*

Do You Have Any Unprofitable Customers?

Maybe you're thinking, "That's fine for a bank, but my business is very different." That's just not the case. No matter what business you're in, the principles we're talking about apply to you. We believe that virtually *every* company in every industry will soon have to reconceive its way of doing business along these lines, with customers at the center. Why? Because the evidence is overwhelming that this is every company's number-one opportunity to create new shareowner wealth, which is something all companies desperately need to do. Consider: Even when the U.S. economy was booming from 1995 to 2000, most of the biggest companies either failed the most basic test of business—they didn't earn their cost of capital—or they passed by the slimmest of margins.

We know for sure that companies did much worse through the slowdown that followed the stock market bust in 2000, despite heavy layoffs, divestitures, and other heroic cost cutting. To put this in the starkest terms: Most companies are failing to achieve what they must achieve to make their share prices rise.

That's a big problem. In trying to solve it, the typical executive looks for troubles in the company's products or business units or territories, which sounds sensible. But that kind of conventional analysis is no longer good enough because it's typically applied to all customers, profitable or not, high potential or low, in the same way. Ever more brutal competition, combined with demanding capital markets and suspicious investors, is challenging managers to rethink their businesses in a fundamentally new way. A number of companies are beginning to do so, using a crucial new insight: If a company's return

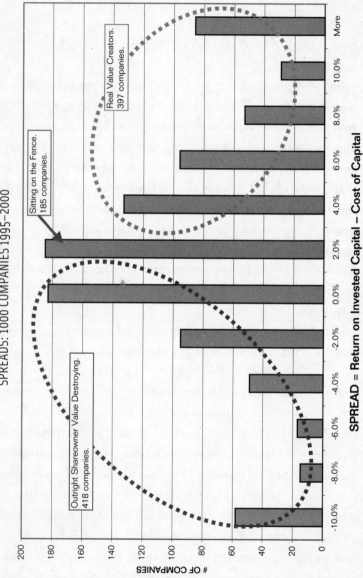

SHAREOWNER VALUE CREATION

SPREADS: 1000 COMPANIES 1995–2000

Real Value Creators.
397 companies.

Sitting on the Fence.
185 companies.

Outright Shareowner Value Destroying.
418 companies.

OF COMPANIES

SPREAD = Return on Invested Capital – Cost of Capital

on capital[2] isn't much better than its cost of capital, then its trouble is even deeper than bad products or business units or territories. By definition the company must have a boatload of *unprofitable customers*.

This is a huge idea: A company consists of both profitable and unprofitable customers—angels and potential demons. Some customers are making your company more valuable while some are draining value from it. Not that the demons are bad individuals; frequently they're unprofitable simply because the company doesn't know who they are and is failing to offer them the right value proposition. Similarly, managers may be blissfully unaware of which customers are the all-important angels. Combined, your angels and demons determine your company's value. This doesn't fit the way most managers run and measure—and thus think about—their businesses. Yet it's obvious that all the profits and value of a company come from its profitable, high-potential customers. If your company has a market capitalization of $20 billion, that value depends entirely on the future profitability of your existing customers and your ability to attract and retain profitable new customers in the future. Thus the first of the three most important principles that emerge from our work and that we will come back to again and again:

◆**Principle No. 1:** Think of your company not as a group of products or services or functions or territories, but as a *portfolio of customers.*

We will see in almost endless ways why this perspective is so extraordinarily valuable, but to get a basic sense of it, just answer this question: Does your company have any unprofitable customers?

We recently asked that question of the top executives at one of America's major retailers. (By unprofitable, we meant failing to earn the cost of capital.) Your answer may well be the same as theirs: No. Amazingly, these executives were quite confident they had no unprofitable customers, even though their business overall was failing to earn its cost of capital. If you're baffled by the apparent illogic of this position, well, so were we. Yet this company's leaders insisted that through some dark financial voodoo, millions of profitable customers somehow added up to an unprofitable company.

Our analysis of customer profitability—an exercise they had never conducted and weren't even sure quite how to conduct—showed them they were wrong. The truth, which shocked them, was that some of their customers were deeply unprofitable. Understand the importance of what this meant: Doing business with these customers on current terms was reducing the firm's market capitalization by hundreds or thousands of dollars per customer. Since the company didn't understand these facts, it was aiming marketing efforts at these customers and others like them. So here's how absurd the situation was: This company was actually spending money to bring in customers that were reducing the value of the firm.

If you believe your company has no unprofitable customers, we hope you're right. But experience has shown us that, like the executives of this retailer, you're probably fooling yourself. We've found that most companies have some very unprofitable customers—as well as hugely profitable customers—but managers rarely believe it or know who they are. In fact, as we'll see in later chapters, the bottom 20 percent of customers by profitability can generate losses equal to more than 100 percent of total company profits. Even if you know you have unprofitable customers, you may be clueless what to do about it. ("We can't fire customers, can we?" some managers ask; the answer is that in some cases you can, as we shall explain, though there's almost always a better alternative. Those demons can often be exorcised.) Yet if a company can't figure out a way to earn at least its cost of capital with individual customers or customer segments, it's just a matter of time until its share price gets crushed. These days that's something no company can afford to risk.

But suppose your company is fabulously profitable already. Are you immune to unprofitable customers? We doubt it. We have examined the customer profitability of two of the most profitable companies in North America and found that 10 percent to 15 percent of their customers are hugely unprofitable. So even in these cases, managers have an opportunity to make their company still more profitable.

It's crazy so many managers refuse to believe they lose money on some customers. Wall Street analysts should be all over this issue, digging deeply into the facts of customer profitability at the companies they cover, especially at companies that are failing to earn their cost of capital. Yet most analysts aren't doing so. In fact, two of Wall Street's top-rated food retailing analysts told us unequivocally there are no unprofitable customers at any of the companies they cover. Little did they know: We had performed analyses at some of these very companies and had found, as we find at every company, that some customers were deeply unprofitable. Yet the news wasn't all bad, for we also discovered highly profitable customers at these companies. But the analysts didn't have a clue.

A Better Way to Boost the Share Price

These analysts, like most managers, are missing what we consider the most powerful way to understand the true economics and influence the share price of a company: analyzing the profitability of its portfolio of customers. Here we begin to see the second of the three vital principles that leap out from this work and that will be elaborated much more fully in Chapters 2, 3, and 4:

◆**Principle No. 2:** Every company's portfolio of customers can and must be managed to produce *superior returns for shareowners*—meaning a consistently better than average share price appreciation—not just to produce earnings per share or EBITDA or revenue growth or customer satisfaction or anything else.

This sounds obvious. Why is it so important? Because it truly is a matter of corporate survival, now more than ever. Capital today travels around the globe instantly, continually, relentlessly seeking its best use. Information about your company and everything that affects it is far more widely available than ever in history, and it, too, travels instantly, globally, continually. Every company now gets a daily report card, in the form of its share price, on how it's doing in the worldwide competition to attract capital, and the grading is getting tougher. Even in Japan and Germany, former bastions of what some analysts used to call, admiringly, "patient capital," the party is over. No capital is very patient anymore. Global capital is demanding performance, and companies that don't deliver are finally being forced to do the unthinkable: fire CEOs, reform boards of directors, and face the new music.

This new imperative is truly unavoidable. Even if your company has an eccentric majority owner who just sits at home watching MTV and couldn't care less what his stock is worth, failure to beat the crowd in making it worth more will lead to trouble in the company's day-to-day operations:

> ✓   The best employees, who increasingly want to be paid partially in stock so they can participate in the success they help create, won't want to join a company that lacks a reputation for creating superior returns for shareowners. Further, companies that don't offer stock-based compensation may have a tougher time holding excellent employees; if they're paid only in cash, it's easy to leave for a better deal elsewhere. Without the best employees, the company will only go further downhill.

> ✓   A history of poor value creation makes new capital more expensive to attract, so the company will have a harder time funding research, development, and expansion that will let it serve customers better. As disaffected customers turn elsewhere, the situation gets worse.

⋎   Companies often need to buy other companies in order to acquire technology, customers, or employees and keep them out of competitors' hands. Valuable shares make an excellent currency for such acquisitions, but if a company's shares haven't grown sufficiently in value, then these acquisitions may be too expensive. The company's competitors win these prizes instead, and yet another downward spiral begins.

We hope it's obvious that creating superior returns for shareowners isn't just in the shareowners' interest. It's in everybody's interest. The company that creates tons of shareowner value will employ more people, pay more taxes, and serve more customers—all while enriching shareowners, who nowadays are most likely ordinary citizens who need their pension funds and mutual funds to perform well in order to pay for retirements and college educations. Failing to create superior shareowner value means none of these good things will happen.

Now a number of leading companies—including Dell Computer, Toronto–based Royal Bank, Fidelity Investments, Best Buy, Britain's Tesco, and others—are getting a grip on their portfolio of customers and managing it to build substantial competitive advantages. What they are doing contributes powerfully and quickly to topline growth, profitability, and a rising share price. The risks of not putting customers at the center therefore become unbearable, and companies that don't do it will face an ugly future. Companies that do it ahead of their competitors will position themselves to dominate.

We must declare up front that this isn't easy to do. That's good news and bad news. The bad news is that it will strain your organization and require a lot of work. The good news is that it will probably be just as hard for your competitors. The even better news is that putting customers at the center offers significant first-mover advantages. So if you can do it first, your company may be able to establish competitive advantages that will last an extraordinarily long time.

Why You're Not Really
Customer Centered

What we're asserting here is much more far-reaching than you may be tempted to think. We can hear you (or your boss) objecting: "We already do this!" The fact is most managers will insist they already put customers at the center. "We put our customers first!" and "We're committed to our customers' success!" claim virtually all companies. Indeed, *customer centric* is one of the loudest business buzzwords of the era. One of America's largest retailers, which we'll identify in a moment, claimed in 2001 to have just three "strategic imperatives," one of which was "creating a customer-centric culture to better satisfy and serve our customers." A Wall Street analyst reports that one of this retailer's top executives told him at the time, "We have a heightened sense of urgency and a clear focus on the customer, and we are working as one unified team to make retail history!" Which retailer was this? It was Kmart. We have to admit the firm did make retail history: In 2002 it filed the largest bankruptcy petition of any retailer, ever.

The claims of customer centricity at most companies are an outright fraud. These companies don't put customers at the center—not really, not as if they truly mean it, not like we're talking about. If you doubt that, ask three questions:

1. Who in the company "owns" the customer? That is, which one, specific, identifiable person is responsible for understanding a designated customer or customer segment thoroughly, for figuring out those customers' total needs and desires, and for figuring out and executing a value proposition that meets them better than the competition, driving the share price as a result? At most companies the answer is: no one. Or rather, more insidiously, the proudly declared answer is, "Lots of people own the customer!" But when a number of people have responsibility for any given customer, the truth is that nobody owns him. Probably not one of those people is responsible for the customer on behalf of the whole company. Instead, each probably represents only a part of it, most likely a product or a function or a territory. Employees in any of those organizational areas may say they own a given customer, but they can't *all* own him. In fact, they are responsible only for those needs and desires of the customer that happen to intersect with the employee's area of the organization. Does this arrangement seem logical? It does to the vast majority of companies everywhere, which are organized in exactly this way. Just remember that it is precisely what got the Bank of Outer Mongolia into so much trouble.

2. Who is accountable for the profitability of any given customer or customer segment? Again, the answer is usually: no one. In fact, as we will see in shocking detail very soon, most companies don't even know how profitable any customer is. It's ludicrous to claim you've put customers at the center if you don't know which ones are making you money and which ones are costing you money, and no one is in charge of managing profitability through creating, communicating, and executing value propositions.

3. How significantly does the company differentiate its interaction with different customers? Companies that put customers at the center don't treat them all the same. On the contrary: These companies understand the importance of a mutually beneficial value exchange, treating different customers very differently because they know that customers have widely varying needs and desires. Meeting these needs better than competitors offers the company the opportunity for earning superb profits, thus turbo-charging its stock. To treat all customers the same makes no sense—yet many companies try hard to do just that and even try to claim that it's a virtue.[3]

For most companies, answering these questions in a customer-centered way amounts to a deep reconception of how they do business. It's a real mind bender for many business people, but the companies doing it are hardly the ones you'd think of as radical.

Royal Bank is 138 years old and has 10 million customers. Dell Computer is the world's largest maker of personal computers. Fidelity Investments is one of the world's largest sellers of mutual funds. The surprising fact is that many of the companies at the leading edge of a clear trend toward putting customers at the center are big, established—and producing spectacular results.

Remember Where the Money Comes From

Putting customers at the center has always made sense for a simple reason that seems so obvious it wouldn't be worth saying except that managers continually forget it: *Customers are where the money comes from.* We will return to this simple but profound truth a number of times because it is, after all, the ultimate reason for putting customers at the center. Ignoring it will almost always get a manager into trouble, if only because it will render him unable to maximize profitability.

Consider: If your company is organized around products, then top management makes decisions based on measures of product revenue or product profitability. But that is not really what management most needs to know. Why? A major retailer with which we worked was earning a handsome profit selling certain dresses to Customer A and losing money selling those very same dresses to Customer B. The reason was that Customer B demanded an enormous amount of the salesperson's time, made lots of returns, was always unhappy with alterations, causing rework, and always paid her house charge account promptly—a potential demon. If the retailer had known this, it might have found ways to turn that demon into a profitable angel, perhaps by discouraging returns ("Let's make *sure* this is the right size, shall we?"), by offering a broader selection of sizes to replace problems with alterations, or by offering the customer highly profitable products (shoes, handbags, belts) that would logically go with the dresses but that she hasn't been buying.

Most companies, however, amalgamate all their financial data into a measure of product revenue or profitability. As a result, the clueless product manager in charge of those dresses just keeps trying to sell more of them, and her efforts—repositioning the garments on the sales floor, motivating sales and alteration people, running advertising, and sending out mass direct mailings—may very well cause Customer B to continue behaving in an unprofitable way, dragging profits further downward. Because product managers typically have no idea which customers are profitable and which ones aren't, they waste lots of resources on the wrong products and customers and leave vast amounts of money on the table by not fully meeting customers' needs.

The benefits of putting customers at the center go far beyond fixing unprofitable customers. When accountable operating executives focus on customer segments rather than on products, functions, or territories, their behavior changes. Rather than just trying to sell more of the product or service for which they're responsible, they try to fulfill more of the customer's total needs. In the previous retail example, the accountable executive focuses on customer segments. She may discover that some of the highest profit potential customers may be petite Asian women who require extensive, expensive alterations due to lack of appropriate sizes. Fixing this problem could easily spark huge increases in profitability through lower costs and increased revenue.

Rather than trying only to take product market share away from direct competitors, managers try also to capture more of specific customers' total spending. Their perspective—and the company's opportunities for profit—expand enormously. This observation leads us to the third of our three vital principles:

▶**Principle No. 3:** Companies enhance customer profitability and drive their stock by creating, communicating, and executing competitively dominant customer value propositions.

Consider our bank customer. For the Bank of Outer Mongolia, this story is even more tragic than it first appears. Not only does this customer trade lots of securities through the bank's brokerage operation, he also does loads of trading through other institutions as well. He maintains big cash balances at the bank but also elsewhere. He buys insurance, but not through the bank. Someday soon he will need trust services. He'd like technical help getting his whole financial life on-line and would be happy to pay for it, but he doesn't even know where to start. In short: *huge* opportunities for the bank.

Needless to say, no one at the bank knew any of this. Yet someone there *could* have known all of it and more, either through third-party data sources or simply by paying attention to the customer. (For example, just knowing how much money he made by trading should have tipped off managers that he wasn't keeping all his cash balances with the bank.) Armed with this knowledge about the customer's specific needs, the relative importance of these needs, and the degree to which competitors were meeting them, the bank could have put together a knockout customer-value proposition to attract all of this customer's financial services business: lower commissions and faster execution on his trades, lower interest rates charged on his margin debt, higher interest rates paid on his cash deposits, a better deal on his mortgage, lower premiums on his insurance, technical help getting his finances on-line, and trust planning—the customer would have been better off in every way. We're well aware that if it isn't careful, the bank could discount itself to a loss. But in this case the bank could have been much better off because it could have more total business and more total profit from this customer even after allowing for discounts. Indeed, if the customer's primary need was saving time—one-stop shopping with a single, high-quality point of contact—discounts might not have been needed. His relationship with the bank would be so deep that competing banks would find it almost impossible to pry him loose. Because the bank would know him so well, it could offer him products and services tailored to his needs, on which the margins would likely be substantial. The customer would be such a fan of the bank that he'd help generate new business through friends, family, and business associates. The bank would be more profitable immediately and for years in the future.

But of course none of this happened.

This customer went to the head of the bank's retail operations. He called him and told him this story. Yes, said the executive, it sounded all too familiar. He'd love to do something about the situation. Trouble was, every idea for addressing the problem seemed to take power away from the managers who ran the product fiefdoms—mortgages, brokerage, etc.—so they found ways to kill every proposal. Because this bank puts *products* at the center, not customers, it never came within a million miles of realizing its huge opportunity with this customer or the thousands like him. Nor does it even realize how awful its performance is, since it measures itself against other similarly awful institutions and therefore thinks it's doing fine. Heaven help it if Royal Bank ever comes to its turf.

Why This Is a Mind Bender

The advantages of being truly customer centered are so large and so clear that one has to ask: Why didn't most companies do this long ago?

Part of the answer is precedent and habit. In an earlier economy, most businesses were based on physical assets—mines, factories, ships, rail lines. Creating all these things required enormous amounts of financial capital, and the capital providers—lenders and equity holders—understandably wanted a careful accounting of how their investments were performing. For financial reporting purposes, it seemed most convenient and logical to match up a mine or factory with the product it produced, a ship or rail line with the territory it served. So the managers of a nineteenth-century industrial conglomerate might report to the owners that bricks (i.e., the brick factory) had a profit of $400,000 and Latin America (i.e., the Honduran rail-road) had a loss of $200,000. Then as now, what gets measured gets managed. Thus grew up a system of managing companies on the basis of products made, functions carried out, and territories served.

So ubiquitous did this practice become that it pervaded, and still pervades, companies that did not have to use it. A small retailer, such as a convenience store, corner deli, or dry cleaner, may be financed entirely by its proprietor and may have only a small number of cus-tomers. For this business, putting customers at the center would not be too tough. The dry cleaner should find it easy to offer pickup, de-livery, and expedited service to its most profitable or highest-potential customers. Yet it rarely happens, simply because the mind-set is miss-ing; our business history and culture don't lead us in that direction. A boutique investment bank, though far larger, is similar: It may be fi-nanced entirely by its partners and have relatively few customers. But most investment banks are organized around products—equities and fixed income, for example—rather than customers. An industrial firm that serves major automakers has only a handful of customers, so put-ting customers at the center would not be technically difficult. It's just a matter of the all-important mind-set.

For many modern businesses of any size, putting customers at the center has also been a huge practical problem, which is another reason it hasn't happened. For any company with lots of customers, the data demands could be overwhelming. If your company has ten products and a million customers, which would you organize around? The products, obviously. Even if you could classify the customers into a manageable handful of segments, the challenges of collecting and handling data about each customer so that each could be assigned to the proper segment—and repeating the exercise for every customer every month or even more often—have in the past been almost insur-mountable. The problems of simply tracking the behavior of large numbers of customers who may interact with the firm through vari-ous channels—by phone, by mail, on-line, in person—can be huge.

Aggregating that data so it could be sliced and diced usefully was another monster challenge. Extracting the data you wanted and then analyzing it were separate, complicated tasks.

But now, in just the past few years, the practical challenges have been met. At long last, computer technology now enables companies to do everything they must do in order to be truly customer centered. For business this is a wonderful, historic development. The trouble is it leads managers to believe that the challenge they face is adopting the technology. It isn't. What many companies are discovering, to their grave disappointment, is that this remarkable technology by itself does not lead them to create significant new value. Many companies have spent millions on the needed software—including ERP (enterprise resource planning), CRM (customer relationship management), and many other applications—with little or nothing to show. What they are finding is that this new technology, like many important new technologies of the past, requires them to do something even harder than spit out numbers or make software work: It demands that they rethink the way they run their businesses. Specifically, it requires them to shift corporate power and redesign business processes as they face the inevitability of putting customers at the center.

An analogy: When electricity came to industry, it was used first to power traditional craft-based forms of work. Efficiency increased somewhat—but then visionaries (such as Henry Ford and Frederick Taylor) saw how this new technology enabled work to be reorganized fundamentally, and wealth creation exploded.

Similarly, when computer technology came to business, first in back-office applications, companies applied it to existing processes and achieved modest gains in efficiency. But then some saw how processes could now be reorganized—for example, by combining ordering, billing, and shipping into a single process—and they achieved breakthroughs in productivity.

Now we have technology that enables companies to manage customer data, and all the associated financial information, in ways that weren't possible even a few years ago. Once again we see most companies applying this new technology to existing conventional processes, generally in sales and marketing, within a conventional structure centered on products, functions, or territories. If these companies are very lucky, they get incrementally better results. But the pioneers are realizing how this technology enables a profound reconception of the business—with customers at the center—leading to breakthrough advances in competitiveness and value creation. It's this reconception, built around the shift in mind-set of putting customers at the center, not the technology, that's most important.

Waking Up from the Technology Dream

Weren't we all supposed to be getting rich through customer knowledge by now? For business, this was a major part of the great promise of the Info Age: At last we would really be able to know about our customers, no matter how many, really keep track of all their interactions with us, and know much more through information from third-party providers, all of it combining seamlessly, constantly, in real time. The payoff? We'd know exactly what every customer wanted—products, services, whatever—and would amaze and delight them with our uncannily on-target offerings. They'd love us. They'd happily pay prices that translated into fantastic margins for us, they'd never leave, and they'd tell all their friends. We'd make so much money and be so competitively dominant that our stock price would burst through the ceiling. We would be business heroes.

That's no exaggeration of the vision that formed as the capabilities of information technology became apparent. Countless books and articles were written about it, including excellent books like those in the *One to One* series by Don Peppers and Martha Rogers. Plenty of people could see what was becoming possible, and they found it awesome. Terms like *mass customization* and *learning relationship* entered the business vocabulary. Technology was about to revolutionize the way business was conducted and even the way it was conceived.

It's true that many companies have started down the road toward capitalizing on their customer data, often by making breathtakingly large investments in computer hardware and software. But where's the payoff? Think of your own experience. How often—or rather, how seldom—are you amazed and delighted by a company that has offered you a solution to one of your problems before you even asked? How about after you've asked? Overall, has your experience as a consumer or as a business customer improved over the past five years?

We don't know many people who would say yes, but in any case we can take a far more rigorous approach to this important matter. Think of the companies that know the most about you and about millions of other customers—that is, the companies that should be realizing the greatest benefits from their new technology-powered abilities to know and serve customers better. Which companies would they be?

They'd probably include credit card companies. Think of what your primary card issuers know about you: where you travel, when, in what class of service, where you eat, what kind of food you like, what kind of wine you drink, where and when you buy clothes, books, furniture, and probably groceries, prescription drugs, gasoline—their data about you is staggering, when you think about it.

Who else knows a lot about you? How about your mortgage issuer? Think of what you had to disclose to get your mortgage—all the assets you own, their locations, their value, all your debts, all your sources of income, your income tax returns, even the terms of your divorce if you've had one. Other financial services providers similarly know a ton about you.

Now that you've got the hang of it, think of what certain other companies know. Your phone company. The airlines, if you travel a lot. Insurance companies, which serve virtually every business in

America. The biggest companies in these industries are sitting on troves of customer data almost beyond imagining. This is supposed to be their moment. Now that the technology future has arrived, they hold the keys to the kingdom.

That's why the reality of their situation is so stunning. We chose a sample of a dozen leading companies[4] from these info-rich industries (see chart on page 23) and analyzed their performance over the past five years, looking for the payoff where it ultimately counts: in the share price. The stock markets have been up and down over that five-year period, so we looked at a more constant gauge: how the companies' P/E multiples compared with the average multiple of the S&P 500.

Our remarkable finding is that every one of these companies failed to match the S&P 500 average multiple throughout the past five years, usually trailing by a substantial margin.

What's the problem? The managers of these Dismal Dozen companies do not dispute that they are missing a huge bet. In every case we found that they understand quite urgently the need to capitalize on their customer knowledge opportunity as quickly as possible. They have invested heavily in the new technology tools; most of them spend over $1 billion a year on computer technology and services, and some spend over $3 billion. They employ lots of intelligent people.

None of that is what's wrong. Their problem is that *they haven't put customers at the center*. Every one of these companies is still organized around products, functions, and territories. On all three of our tests of customer centricity, they fail:

1. No single individual owns the customer.
2. No one is accountable for customer profitability (and unprofitability).
3. These companies make little effort to differentiate customers and to treat them differently.

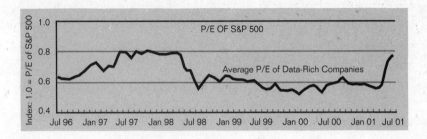

Rather than rethinking their businesses, they're tweaking old processes and customer value propositions, and significant value creation isn't happening.

This cost to shareowners is astonishing. If the Dismal Dozen could simply raise their P/E multiples to the S&P 500 average—that is, if they could really get it together and become mediocre—they would create *a half-trillion dollars* of market capitalization. If they could begin to realize the value in their extraordinary depth of potential customer knowledge, say by achieving P/E multiples as far above the average as they are currently below it—a modest goal, we believe, as the next chapter will make clear—then they would create a trillion dollars of new shareowner value. We will return often to this notion of moving from a discount P/E to a premium P/E.

That is the potential for just these dozen large companies. Think of the potential for the companies with which they compete, virtually none of which are performing much better. Then consider the possibilities for other companies worldwide, all of which possess customer data, have access to more data than they now possess, and are probably realizing little of the opportunity it holds. When we call this a trillion-dollar opportunity, it's clear we are being conservative in the extreme. The true opportunity is much, much larger. And it is *your* opportunity, whether your business is manufacturing, services, or information, whether you sell to businesses or individuals—no company is exempt.

Managing, Measuring, Strategizing in a New Way

Start imagining all the ways a company with deep customer knowledge could please customers, and the endless possibilities make you almost light-headed. But forget about the blue-sky possibilities. What's really striking are all the simple, obvious things that still aren't being done. Consider:

> ∀   The front cabin of an airliner is filled with a variety of customers. Some may be infrequent travelers who bought a low-fare coach ticket and are using an upgrade given to them by a family member. Others may be business fliers who pay full fare and travel across the country and back every week. The airline knows which is which and logically should want to make sure the high-profit customers get their first choice of seat, meal, wine, etc. Yet it almost never happens, meaning the airlines often—and needlessly—tick off their most valuable customers.

> ∀   A phone company offers DSL (digital subscriber line) service in the same way to all its customers: by sending them a kit with which to install the service themselves. But the company knows, through a customer's name or monthly bill size, which customers are small businesses or other heavy consumer users who are likely to be especially busy and willing to pay for installation. Since the company has an army of technicians in vans, offering the service to just the right customers

needn't be a problem and could be highly profitable. Yet many major telcos haven't grabbed this opportunity despite the rapid commoditization of their businesses and plummeting P/E ratios.

∀   When you slide your bank card into an ATM, the machine instantly knows a huge amount about you, yet it acts as if it never heard of you. It knows that on 98 percent of your visits over the past two years, you've withdrawn $200 in cash from your checking account. It could ask immediately if that's what you'd like to do this time, but instead it runs you through the same menu as every other customer. While you're waiting for it to check your account and disburse the cash, the screen tries to sell you the bank's Visa card—even though it knows you already have one. It also knows you have no home equity line of credit with the bank, but it makes no attempt to sell you that.

∀   Even small retailers possess valuable but unused customer data. A restaurant owner knows—though he may never have dug through his data to figure out—which customers most often order expensive wine, the most profitable item any restaurant sells. Through further analysis of the information, the restaurateur can approach these customers in many ways: by notifying them of special offers of their favorite foods or of seasonal foods, by offering late-notice reservations at the busiest times, by assuring them of their favorite table or server, or by offering particular high-end wines that aren't on the wine list. It isn't complicated, but most restaurants don't do it.

By now you realize what the problem is. Because of history and habits, most managers behave as if profit comes from products ("Yogurt is up 13 percent this year!") or places ("Europe is off this quarter"). But it doesn't. It comes from customers, and facing that reality is a bigger change than most managers realize.

In these examples and in general, note one of the most important attractions of capitalizing on customer data: *It's creating value from what you already have.* As every industry consolidates and becomes more competitive, the pressure to create value only increases, and it isn't going to let up. Every company needs help. In these circumstances it feels like a gift to discover that you have a valuable "new" asset that in fact has been sitting there all along, underused because the company wasn't organized to optimize it.

Corporate managers aren't the only ones thinking more about the value of this asset. Investors are too. In fact, a blue-ribbon task force created at the request of former Securities and Exchange Commission Chairman Arthur Levitt found that investors increasingly want information about companies' customer-knowledge assets as an aid in evaluating companies. The task force urged the government to "take as many actions as it can" to create an environment that encourages companies to disclose such information as the loyalty of its customers, changes in its customer acquisition costs, and changes in its revenue per customer, none of which need be reported under current rules. In our view it's essential that companies get a handle on customer knowledge not just to compete for business in the product and service markets, but also to compete for investors' money in the capital markets. This becomes obvious once you think of a company's share price as the sum of customer segment values.

Putting customers at the center will also help overcome one of the largest business problems of recent years, the high failure rate of mergers and acquisitions. We have just gone through the biggest M&A (mergers and acquisitions) wave in history, with acquiring companies paying huge premiums to get their targets, but most of these deals don't pay off for shareowners. Why not? The most common justification for deals today is cost synergies, but they rarely yield much benefit for the acquirer's shareowners because these savings are easy to estimate ahead of time and in practice end up getting negotiated away as a price concession to the selling company. The buyer typically pays a huge margin above the value of the acquiree's tangible assets, a difference that accountants call goodwill as a catchall term for the company's intangible assets. In practice, the most valuable of those intangible assets is the value of the acquired company's profitable or high-potential customers, which represent significant new profit potential. Yet it's extremely rare for an acquiring company to focus on realizing that value by intensively mining the gold in the acquired customer data, and even rarer for it to develop and combine both companies' customer knowledge assets. Instead, most buyers just whale away at cost cutting and whine about incompatible legacy computer systems. As we'll show in Chapter 10, most companies would serve their shareowners far better if they approached M&A with customers at the center. During the historic M&A wave just concluded, in which deal volume exceeded $12 trillion, we estimate this approach could have saved shareowners at least $1 trillion—another $1-trillion opportunity, on top of the one already described. It could also have avoided some severe customer dissatisfaction and needless, ineffective layoffs of hardworking employees.

If it sounds as if we're saying most companies are just plain clueless, we aren't. Our research at dozens of major companies shows that many managers understand the immensity of the customer knowledge opportunity and want desperately to begin realizing it. Managers know they're leaving enormous amounts of wealth on the table. In every industry we've cited, virtually all companies have launched programs to create more value from their customers. But because most of these companies haven't placed customers at the center by following the three key principles—thinking of their companies as a portfolio of customers, managing the portfolio for share price appreciation, and creating, communicating, and executing dominant customer value propositions—their programs aren't doing very well.

Rate Your Readiness

We have developed a framework for realizing these new opportunities that is unlike any you have seen before. It brings together three key concepts that will appear time and again throughout the book:

1. *A premium P/E multiple as the measure of success.* Never forget that the bottom-line goal of every business is to create superior returns for shareowners. As markets rise and fall over time, a premium P/E is your constant assurance that you're exceeding the average and achieving that goal. Specifically, it shows that investors acknowledge your superior ability to create value now and into the future.

2. *Value Proposition Management (VPM).* This is a new way of thinking about the process of using customer data to deliver vastly improved customer value propositions and thus create and sustain a premium P/E. Not just data mining, not just decision analytics, not just customer relationship management, VPM is a new, hands-on approach to realizing the enormous opportunity in customer data.

3. *Creating a customer-centered enterprise,* characterized by a mind-set, an organizational form, and a culture based on accountability for increasing the share price through customer knowledge. Everyone in business knows that nothing good happens unless someone is accountable for it. We will see repeatedly the importance of creating an organization and culture in which managers are accountable for realizing the potential of customer knowledge. In most companies the required changes will be substantial, but they are worth it. Halfway measures, such as complex and often confusing matrix organizations, suck huge energy out of the workforce. Clear accountability, by contrast, attracts hard-charging managers who want to show they can deliver.

What are the requirements and rewards of this opportunity? Here's an analogy about the potential of laser focus and unrelenting discipline. About six years ago General Electric decided to pursue a six-sigma quality program. Many other companies had adopted such programs, with varying success. GE realized that the only point of such a program is to create returns for shareowners, and realized also that it would never succeed without total commitment. So the company, using elements of six-sigma quality analysis that were generally available, created its own program that involved every employee. No manager could be promoted without six-sigma training, and every manager was held accountable for creating value through six sigma. Today, after spending hundreds of millions on training, technology, and operationalizing, GE has produced over $5 billion of new profits beyond the required investments.[5]

The point is that GE didn't invent six sigma. It didn't have to. The pieces were there, waiting to be put together. What GE did was assemble them and apply them with total commitment, making managers accountable for the results.

We believe that the shareowner value potential of putting customers at the center is at least as great as six sigma. It is now, finally, a practical goal: The pieces are there, waiting to be assembled and applied. It's time for visionary leaders to make their move. Doing so will require intense focus and discipline. The good news is that the benefits can begin to be realized quite quickly.

Our analysis of successes and failures in realizing the potential of the data gold mines that many companies are sitting on shows that winning requires effectively addressing the needs of customers, shareholders, and employees. To do so, every company needs a strong foundation made of seven leadership elements. All seven are required; a missing one, like a missing stone in a foundation, will lead to certain trouble. The seven are highly interdependent. A few fortunate companies have possessed some of these elements for decades—a powerful competitive advantage, and all the more reason for other companies to start building right away.

As we describe the elements, ask which ones your company has, needs to build, or needs to strengthen. Ask yourself what's in it for your customers, shareowners, and employees. Give your company a score of zero to ten on each trait. Many managers find it valuable to score their most threatening competitor as well. At the end we'll explain what your total means.

1. Your leadership is committed to delivering and maintaining a premium P/E multiple.

2. Your company organizes strategic planning around customer segments—with a cultural belief that not all customers should be treated identically.

3. Your company has a truly customer-centered mind-set and a corporate organization built around customer segments, each with a leader bearing full profit-and-loss accountability and concomitant authority to wow the customer and realize the company's financial goals.

4. Your company understands the true profitability of its customers and how this determines its stock price and P/E.

5. Your corporate culture has a consistent bias toward creating new winning value propositions by forming hypotheses, then testing, verifying, and executing the results on a major scale.

6. Your company has a record of merging or acquiring business successfully, with zero decline in customer satisfaction and significant increases in customer knowledge among the most valuable customer segments.

7. Your top management regularly spends at least 25 percent of its time teaching these principles to all levels of the organization.

Now add up your score. Here's what the total means:

0–25   Like most companies, you're a long way from raising your stock price by putting customers at the center. Focus first on taking the baby steps that will get your total up.

26–50   You're getting there. With a score in this range, you're probably doing a few things very well. The key now is to improve your lowest scores quickly.

51–70   You're far ahead of most companies. Go for it. The management challenges won't be easy, but you're better prepared for them than most. Move now, and you could build a strong competitive advantage with your customers and deliver a consistent premium P/E for your shareowners.

If you don't score well, don't despair. Few companies get high scores, which means the opportunity for you is great. In addition, since fully capturing this opportunity is difficult, the first-mover advantage is unquestionably significant.

The first movers are already putting distance between themselves and their product-, territory-, and function-centered competitors. Turning to them for real-world examples, we'll create a picture of how the many elements of this opportunity can be combined to create a powerful engine of shareowner wealth.

Specifically, we'll show the keys to high scores on each of the questions above:

> ⅄   Question 1: Chapter 4 shows why a premium P/E multiple is so important.
>
> ⅄   Question 2: Chapters 5 and 6 show the value of organizing around customers and differentiating between them.
>
> ⅄   Question 3: Chapter 5 plus Chapters 6 and 9 show the critical importance of mind-set and accountability.
>
> ⅄   Question 4: Chapters 2, 3, and 4 show the surprising ways your customer relationships add to or detract from your company's share price and thus its P/E.
>
> ⅄   Question 5: Chapters 7 and 8 describe how successful companies create, communicate, and execute winning value propositions.
>
> ⅄   Question 6: Chapter 10 presents a new and better approach to mergers and acquisitions.
>
> ⅄   Question 7: Chapters 9 and 11 describe the methods of spreading these ideas throughout an organization.

Let's now take the next step in making your company a winner by understanding more deeply the benefit of putting customers at the center, focusing where it counts most: in sustained profitable growth and the share price.

Don't Buy These Excuses

Managers in every industry can come up with plenty of reasons for not making better use of their extensive customer data—but many of their excuses aren't valid. Among those we've heard most:

"The privacy issues are too tough."

As long as a company is using its own data or legitimately purchased third-party data, privacy issues are rarely significant. More important is how much the customer expects the company to know: A consumer may be jolted to receive an offer suggesting that his credit card company knows the size of his mortgage, though that information may be easily and legitimately available. An advantage for big financial services firms is that customers expect them to know a lot.

"We're in a regulated industry."

Government regulations may prevent certain moves; phone companies, for example, can't differentiate some services by customer profitability. But even then, opportunities to use customer data for creating shareholder value—through cross-selling, up-selling, and offering new products and services—remain plentiful.

"We've already got a lot of customer-focused initiatives."

An insidious excuse, because it suggests that all is well. But all is not well unless those initiatives are expected to realize customer returns on invested capital significantly above the cost of capital, and someone is being held accountable for those results. It's rarely so.

"We're under too much short-term earnings pressure to do it now."

Then you'll never do it—can you think of any company that *isn't* under short-term earnings pressure? If you don't get the process started now, competitors could seize an advantage. When that happens, you'll really get to feel some earnings pressure. It's all about prioritization by leadership.

△ 2 ▽

Will This Customer Sink Your Stock?

Understanding How Your
Average Customer Creates or
Destroys Shareowner Value

How do you think of your company? As a collection of people? As a group of offices or factories? As an array of products and services or a collection of divisions and departments? It can be all these things—but for managers focused on making the stock go up and for everyone touching the customer, a company is above all a portfolio of customers.

This is a radical notion; it simply isn't how most managers and investors conceive of a company. Yet the reason for our view is simple common sense. Remember: *Customers are where the money comes from.* If we want to analyze and manage the company as a creator of shareowner wealth, measured in dollars, then we'll find it most useful to view the company as a collection of sources of dollars, and those sources are customers—nothing else. Until we understand the company at this level, we don't really understand how value is being created, or, all too often, destroyed. Once we embrace the concept of the company as a portfolio of customers, we immediately face a number of new, extremely important, and often baffling questions. The most important questions arise from the obvious fact that the value of the company, the thing every manager is supposed to maximize, is the aggregated value of all the customers. So: What is the value of a particular customer, or a group of customers forming a segment? Can a customer's value really be calculated? If it can, how can I as a manager affect that value?

Further critically important questions cascade from this premise by the dozen. For example, which customers, current or potential, are attractive and which are not? How can I attract additional valuable customers? How much should I spend on attracting, serving, and knowing them? How can I make my unprofitable customers more profitable? What if I spent less—or more—on customer service? Am I better off attracting customers who spend a little every year for many years, or customers who spend a lot for a few years and then leave?

For a company with a $50-billion market capitalization, these can be multibillion-dollar questions. The way a manager answers them and many related questions will directly and powerfully affect the value of the company, for better or worse. And in fact managers answer these questions every day when they make decisions on marketing, customer service, sales, technology, capital spending, mergers, organizational structure—but they may not know they are answering these vital questions, and in nearly all cases they are answering on intuition or just plain guesswork. As a result, they are inevitably failing to maximize the value of their shares and may even be driving their stock down.

It is possible for managers to answer these questions quite rigorously and thus push their stock upward far more powerfully than they are doing today. The results are often surprising. They are based on data that most companies already possess but just aren't using, or could get easily through sampling. And why don't they do this? Because it has simply never occurred to them. They don't think of the company as a portfolio of customers—or maybe they've thought about it, but their organizational structure makes trying it too daunting. As we work our way through these analyses and you start to think about performing them at your company, don't forget: The necessary data is almost certainly there, waiting to be turned into knowledge and used in ways that will make the company's stock worth more.

This chapter is about *applying* the first two of the three big principles we introduced in Chapter 1. Every company is a portfolio of customers, and management's job is to manage the portfolio so as to maximize the company's share price over time. We'll begin to explain how a company can raise its share price significantly by understanding customer finances. The ensuing discussion about the economics of the *average* customer will prepare us for the next critical step, understanding how to figure out the distribution of profitability across *different* customers.

What the Average Customer Is Really Worth

How much shareowner value does a customer create? One way to answer that question is through a top-down approach—that is, by starting with a company's total value, which by definition must be the aggregated value of all its customers. Consider Capital One Financial, which is one of America's largest issuers of Visa and MasterCard credit cards. As of the beginning of 2002 Capital One had a total market value of about $11.7 billion.[1] But that's not the amount of shareowner wealth it had created. After all, investors had to put capital into the company, so the company has created wealth only to the extent it is worth more than the amount of capital that was put into it. This is a critically important idea that a great many people, including people who should know better, often forget. By this measure Capital One had, at that time, performed extremely well: Only about $4.3 billion of capital was invested in the business, so the company's shareowner value created was $11.7 billion minus $4.3 billion, or about $7.4 billion.[2]

Now, value creation per customer: Capital One had 43.8 million customers at the time of these figures. The average shareholder value creation per customer is thus easy to calculate; it's $169. Note that this is *not* profit per customer. Nor is it market capitalization per customer. It's a much more important and more demanding measure: the amount of wealth Capital One created for its shareowners with each customer, on average.[3]

Such a figure is meaningful for Capital One because its customers are relatively homogeneous: They're all individual credit-card holders, though they differ widely in creditworthiness, behavior, and needs. By contrast, average customer value would not be a very meaningful figure for, say, IBM, whose customers range from individuals buying a laptop computer to giant companies spending hundreds of millions of dollars on mainframes, software, and consulting.

As we will see in the next chapter, averages can be a dangerous trap when analyzing customer-based financial measures. Going beyond the averages—distinguishing value-creating customers from value destroyers—is a crucial task that most companies are not performing. And even for Capital One, the average customer value figure reflects a wide range of customers: some who are extraordinarily valuable, others who are actually destroying value, and many others in between.[4]

Still, with that caution understood, even this elementary average customer value analysis can be enlightening and sometimes alarming for many companies whose customers are of similar type. To see what it can reveal—for better or for worse—consider the example of AT&T Wireless, the cellular service company spun off from AT&T.

AT&T Wireless should be applauded for publishing fairly detailed data about its customer finances—customer acquisition costs, number of customers, churn rate, and other important figures. What they reveal, however, is not encouraging. As of early 2001, AT&T

Wireless had 18 million customers. The company's total enterprise value was $31 billion. But remember, to find how much shareowner value the company had created, we must subtract from this figure the total capital invested in the business. For AT&T Wireless, this figure was $38.3 billion.

This is not good: The total invested capital was *greater* than the total market value of the company. Thus, far from creating shareowner value at all, AT&T Wireless had actually destroyed it, to the tune of $7.3 billion, or $406 per customer. That is, AT&T Wireless's per-customer value creation was minus $406.[5]

The company reported that acquiring customers cost it about $335 each, and it held them for about three years on average. We can combine this information with other data from the company's financial statements—we won't take you through the somewhat involved math—to calculate what the company would have to achieve just to stop destroying shareowner value. The answer is that, if other factors remained unchanged, it would have to increase annual revenues by $231 per customer! That's almost $20 per month for each of its 18 million customers on average—a plausible goal in some industries, but probably not in the cutthroat cellular business, where brutal competition means prices are continually falling. And remember, even if the company could achieve this extremely ambitious goal, it still wouldn't be creating a dime of shareowner value. It would simply have stopped destroying its shareowner wealth. Perhaps it's little wonder that the company's stock continued to fall for many months after we performed this analysis.

We hope you agree that the results of this customer profitability analysis would have been enormously useful to many investors contemplating the future of AT&T Wireless, and to the company's managers, who could have seen that incremental progress was just not going to turn the firm into a winner, and that some kind of radical change in approach was their only hope of achieving what they're paid to do.

In fact, however, most corporate leaders we've interviewed, across a wide spectrum of industries, don't even know their average value creation per customer—their companies' equivalent of the $169 for Capital One or the minus $406 for AT&T Wireless.

All About Eva and Her Value

As useful as that kind of top-down average customer analysis can be, it is only the beginning of what managers can and must know about customer finance. Taking the next step, they can use a bottom-up approach to calculate a far more revealing figure: not an average, but the value of a specific customer.

To illustrate the concepts most clearly, let's consider a hypothetical company, which we'll call Multimax. It could be in any kind of business, including yours. If the numbers we use don't seem appropriate to your company, then multiply or divide them; the principles won't change. We can assure you from experience that the example is quite realistic.

First we'll do a top-down analysis like the ones we've done already. Multimax has a total enterprise value of $1.536 billion— today's total market value of all the company's equity and debt. Total capital invested in the business is $1 billion. The difference between those two figures, $536 million, is the total wealth created by the company. Multimax has 1 million customers, so its average wealth creation per customer is simple to calculate: It's $536.

The trouble with this average, top-down figure is that it isn't very actionable. Managers don't know *which* customers are worth $536, or which are worth more, which less, so they don't know exactly what to do in order to make the number go up. But they can know. To see how, let's use a bottom-up approach to find the value of one particular Multimax customer, whom we'll call Eva. And while we're using a hypothetical example to keep the numbers simple, the fact is that a number of companies, such as RBC Royal Bank, Dell Computer, and

Fidelity Investments, actually calculate the value of particular customers in just this way, and you can too.

To find out how much Eva is worth to Multimax, we must first figure how much profit the company earns from her in a year. But we're not interested in profit the way companies have traditionally calculated it. Rather, we want to know how much *economic profit* the company earns from Eva, because this is the measure of profit that translates most directly into the stock price. Economic profit is simply after-tax operating profit after an appropriate charge for capital. It has become a familiar concept to most managers over the past decade as they have realized how important it is. It has been popularized and explained particularly by the Stern Stewart consulting firm, which calls it Economic Value Added.

With regard to a huge company or a single customer, economic profit is calculated in the same way. We'll explain it conceptually here with regard to Multimax and Eva, without worrying about the nitty-gritty of how companies extract some of these numbers from their financial statements. Don't worry, though, we'll get to that eventually.

⋎   First we see how much of Multimax's invested capital is attributable to Eva.[6] Such capital could include the equipment used to make the products Eva buys, or the branch office she visits, or her receivables (the amount of money she owes the company). For purposes of economic profit, it also includes investments that aren't counted as capital under normal accounting rules but that really are capital, since they represent money spent today that is intended to pay off years down the road. These could include the costs of developing the products Eva buys or training the people who serve her. When all these things are appropriately weighted, let's say Multimax has a nice, round $1,000 of capital attributable to Eva.

⋎   Next we look at how much money Multimax earned on Eva's capital as shown by a common measure of profitability called net operating profit after tax.[7] (We will always consider these figures on an annual basis, though you could use any period of time.) Multimax earns $350 from Eva.

Ⅴ   Since the company earned $350 on $1,000 of invested capital, it has a return on invested capital of 35%.

Ⅴ   Next we see how much the capital cost. Multimax's cost of capital is 10%, a typical figure.

Ⅴ   The difference between return on invested capital and cost of capital is what we call the spread. In this case it is 35% minus 10%, or 25%. The concepts of capital cost and return on invested capital contain some subtleties we'll get into later, but the basic notions are intuitive and familiar. The big idea here, arguably the most fundamental idea in business, is that a company has to earn a greater return on its capital than the capital cost. That is precisely what it means to create wealth. If a company earns less than its capital cost, as many companies do, then it is destroying shareowner wealth. Despite the bedrock importance of this notion, it is amazing how many business people ignore it or forget it.

Ⅴ   Finally we multiply the spread by the capital, or in this case 25% by $1,000. The result, $250, is the economic profit Multimax earns from Eva in a year. To repeat, this isn't just theory. Real companies calculate this figure. They use it to spot where to improve value propositions for existing customers and to identify customers they should try to acquire, and at what cost. Royal Bank, for example, calculates the economic profitability of every one of its 10 million customers every month.

That $250 figure, the company's economic profit from Eva in a single year, is crucial in calculating Eva's total value to the company, which we can now figure. To calculate how much shareowner value an entire company has created, investors need to estimate the company's annual economic profit for years into the future and then discount those amounts back to the present at an appropriate rate. (For the quantitatively inclined, that rate is the cost of capital.) To figure the value of a given customer like Eva, we do exactly the same thing.

Let's say Multimax believes, based on experience, that it will earn $250 of economic profit from Eva every year for ten years, after which she will cease to be a customer. To find Eva's value, we discount that stream of future economic profits back to the present. The result is $1,536—the present value of all the future economic profits from Eva, discounted back to the present at 10 percent a year. Finally, we add one more assumption: that in the year before Eva does any business with Multimax, the company spends $1,000 to acquire her as a customer. So we subtract that acquisition cost ($1,000) from the present value of the future economic profits from Eva ($1,536) to get $536. This is the shareowner value Eva creates for Multimax.

In practice, can a company really calculate this number the way Multimax did? Absolutely. What many managers suspect will be the hardest part—figuring the profitability of a given customer—is well within the capabilities of any company. Arranging internal processes to get the right data to the right place may require the organization to stretch some muscles it didn't know it had, but it's all doable. Customer duration, the period over which a customer earns a return over the cost of capital (ten years in this example), is necessarily a forecast, but it can be estimated from the company's experience. And the CFO already knows the company's capital cost.[8] Those are all the factors you need.

So Eva just happens to be an average Multimax customer. Her particular value, $536, is the same as Multimax's average shareowner value per customer calculated by the top-down approach. We constructed the example in this way to make the concepts clear. In practice, of course, different customers will have widely differing values, any of which we can calculate, and the import can prove to be staggering.

Now let's take the final step. You'll recall we said Multimax has a market cap of $1.536 billion.[9] If we suppose it has 100 million shares outstanding, then its stock is selling for $15.36 a share. And Multimax's managers, for the first time in their lives, can now see exactly how a change in the value of *any customer* will affect the price of the stock.

The careful reader will have noted that we made a simplifying assumption in the discussion above. We assumed Multimax consists of a million Evas, all of whom will cease to be customers in ten years. That could mean the company will suddenly vaporize in a decade, which of course isn't very realistic. Or, for the same result, it could mean that in ten years competitors figure out how to match or beat Multimax's value proposition, competing the company's return on capital down to the cost of capital, 10 percent, so no shareowner value is being created. That's more realistic. But if we assume instead that every disappearing Eva gets replaced by an identical one—that Multimax is in effect a steady state of a million Evas—then the stock price would become much more impressive. And were we to assume that Multimax could actually grow—that is, could increase its economic profit year after year by increasing its total customers or getting more economic profit from each one, or both—then the price would be higher still.

If you can calculate the value of a given customer or customer segment, you hold a highly significant advantage over 99 percent of your competitors. The reason is that once you have the framework for figuring the value of a customer, you possess *actionable* information that most self-proclaimed customer-centric companies don't have. For example, one of the most important elements in Kmart's unsuccessful efforts to become more customer-centered was its Super Service Index score, which was a highly ambitious program of surveying customers about their satisfaction. Trouble was, Kmart could only guess about why satisfaction levels rose or fell. Even more important, managers didn't know which customers were satisfied and which were not. Was the company delighting hordes of unprofitable customers and ticking off a smaller number of highly profitable angel customers? If so, its Super Service Index score would have risen (which it did), while its stock price would have tanked (which it did). Kmart couldn't even begin to approach this problem because, like most companies, it hadn't the least idea which customers or customer segments were producing an economic profit and which were not, or, most important, why.

We've seen exactly how a company's customer relationships translate into its share price—a critically important understanding, yet one that most managers don't have or even appreciate. Now we're ready to delve more deeply into customer finance to see how *differences* in profitability across customers create huge but largely overlooked opportunities, and to see how managers can take advantage of these opportunities to gain competitive advantage and win with investors.

$\triangle$ 3 $\triangledown$

The Astonishing Truth About Customer Profitability

The Surprising Things You Discover When You Learn How to "Deaverage" It

When we said Multimax earns $350 (net operating profit after tax) on Eva, and that the company has $1,000 of capital allocatable to her, you may have wondered how Multimax would ever know this. After all, your company probably doesn't know the analogous figures for any of its customers; most companies don't. But most managers do immediately see the value of knowing these figures, so they quickly start trying to calculate them so they can act on the insights. That's great—but we've found that business people often go astray on this journey in a few important ways.

In this chapter we'll show the concepts that are most important in figuring customer profitability the right way. Then we'll illustrate the ways so many companies go seriously wrong, making bad decisions and misallocating resources, when they don't truly understand the economic profitability of customers or its impact. We'll also show some further enormous advantages to be gained by applying these concepts properly. At that point, if you're like most of the business-people we work with, you'll be even more eager to start figuring these numbers and gaining valuable insights. The real nuts and bolts of how that's done will be a topic for Chapter 4.

You'll recall the major retailer we mentioned in Chapter 1, the company whose managers insisted that through some bizarre magic they had no unprofitable customers even though their company as a whole was unprofitable. Why did they believe such an apparently il-logical thing? Well, they explained, all their products had positive gross margins, and they managed inventories well, so there wasn't tons of capital tied up. Thus, they figured, all their products were profitable, even on the basis of economic profitability (return on cap-ital exceeding cost of capital). So no matter what bundles of goods customers bought, all the customers must be profitable too.

Trouble was, these managers—like many, including some who claim to analyze customer profitability—were ignoring important costs. As a first pass, think of customer profitability as the sum of the profitability of the products and services the customer buys, adjusted for costs specific to that customer, including capital costs. In the case of this retailer, start with a store's operating expenses: sales associates, rent, electricity, maintenance, and so on. If the shoe department occu-pies 10 percent of the store, or has 10 percent of the customer traffic, it should bear 10 percent of the operating costs. Just by allocating those expenses, the company found that 25 percent of its product categories were unprofitable, and many were very unprofitable. Charges for capi-tal—not just inventories, but also things like store fixtures, improve-ments, leases, or capital investments—are critical as well. As we've discussed, subtracting those capital charges from net operating profit after tax yields economic profit. In this case the company found that more than 50 percent of its product categories were generating nega-tive economic profit! In fact, some had returns on invested capital of negative 25 percent, far below the company's 9 percent cost of capital.

The immediate reaction of the managers, who were shocked by these findings, was to consider dropping the most unprofitable product categories. But as we'll see, that would have been a serious mistake.

Using credit-card data and simple observation in stores, the company learned important facts about customer-specific costs, a cost category that most companies ignore. Managers analyzed bundles of goods bought by a varied sample of customers and found that some customers chronically bought mostly unprofitable products. Those customers were unprofitable. The company also found that some customers made lots of returns, behavior that could turn profitable bundles unprofitable. Others bought only items that were on sale, which could have the same effect; those customers were also unprofitable. Some customers had store credit cards on which they charged large balances and made only the minimum payment every month, which was profitable behavior, but others paid their balances in full every month, which reduced their profitability. Another group of losers were those who tie up sales associates and don't buy anything. Hiding in these data were both demon and angel customers.

This analysis showed further that some customers were highly profitable—and that some of these prize customers regularly bought unprofitable products. For example, some bought unprofitable branded shoes but at the same time also bought high-margin belts, plus accessories such as sunglasses, as well as private label jeans and sweaters in significant quantities, all of which are extremely profitable. So if managers had followed their initial instinct and dropped the most unprofitable product categories, they might have driven away some of the company's best customers who were looking for product bundles. The problem, in other words, was not as simple as unprofitable products. The problem was unprofitable customers.

Most customers are not born unprofitable. Sometimes the problem is that a company can't create a compelling value proposition for a particular customer segment. Sometimes the company sees only a snapshot of a customer's behavior. These customers are not demons in our language. Consider the case of a regular, loyal, full-fare first-class air traveler who can't redeem her frequent flier miles for a vacation trip because the seat was given to an infrequent discount flier who redeems points accumulated on a credit card program. In other cases, by not understanding customer profitability, managers often train customers to be unprofitable. Sales employees may be so eager to close a sale— they are often compensated on exactly that basis—that they encourage the customer to take the wrong size or color—"just return it later if you're not happy." But returns are profit-killers. Promotional discounts and sales flyers are typically sent indiscriminately to everyone; customers who buy only on sale appear to be loyal regulars and are encouraged to continue such behavior. The placement of sale items can also be critical; putting them too close to the cash register can make it too easy for customers to buy the unprofitable item and not make the profitable bundle purchase. A company that has made great progress quantifying the incremental opportunities from changing customer behavior is 332-year-old Hudson's Bay Company of Canada. By combining their credit card and loyalty programs for their Zellers and Hudson Bay stores, they are gaining valuable insights into the huge customer profitability advantages to be realized by changing customer behavior. They know, for example, how changing returns behavior affects the profitability of different segments of customers. This is key in their battle to withstand the attack of Wal-Mart.

We want to be clear that we're not arguing that all customers with negative economic profit are demons and should be "fired" immediately. Certainly some are covering fixed costs and some capital costs. We're saying that management must find ways of earning a positive economic profit from them or *replacing* them with profitable new revenues from existing or new customers. More broadly, resources need to be reallocated to existing and future profitable customers. But as we will see later, some customers are real demons who will have to be dealt with.

In our experience, exactly the same issues of denial and proper accounting for customer profitability arise whether your business is banking, insurance, autos, air travel, food and lodging, or telecommunications, and whether it's large or small.

Specifically, the story of this retailer illustrates one of the most widespread and serious problems companies encounter when they attempt to figure customer profitability: Managers don't want to allocate *all* the company's costs and invested capital to customers. Never mind that each of our best-practice companies, including Royal Bank, Dell, and Fidelity, insists on a full allocation. We've encountered the same objection time and again in explaining customer profitability to managers. At a wireless telephone company, for example, the CFO said "Whoa!" when he saw the direction our analysis was taking. Allocating all costs to customers isn't fair, he said. We've got a big business here that's up and running, so we should analyze customer profitability strictly on an *incremental* basis. For any given customer, we should balance revenues from that customer against only the additional costs (operating costs and capital costs) we have to incur in order to get that business.

Look at it that way, and at most companies every single customer will appear profitable. Bringing in enough revenue to cover incremental costs just isn't very hard. Unfortunately, the logic of this approach is deeply flawed. Okay, we responded to the CFO, but suppose you lose your biggest customer. He's covering a big chunk of your fixed costs, and now those costs aren't being covered anymore. Would you still say that the next customer you bring in the door should be evaluated only on whether he covers your incremental costs? If so, then how will those fixed costs ever get covered? If all revenue comes from customers, then which customer is the source of the revenue to cover those costs? After all, somebody has to be.

The CFO, to his credit, got it. He understood that *all* of the company's costs must be attributed to specific customers because the only way the company continues to exist is by serving customers. Incredible that it even has to be said, isn't it? Yet this CFO's attitude is extremely widespread. For example, we often hear managers object that a certain corporate cost—often an administrative or staff cost—just shouldn't really be allocated among specific customers. It's too far removed from them, and besides, line managers can't control it. To which we reply: *Then why does the company incur that cost?* If it doesn't somehow connect to serving or acquiring or retaining customers, then there's no reason for incurring it. And that means *every* cost. The CEO's private jet? Figure out some basis for allocating it to customers; if you can't, then you can't escape the fact that there's no reason for having it.

Principle One says the company is a portfolio of customers, and you simply can't analyze that portfolio usefully if all the costs aren't allocated. We agree there are certain decisions for which incremental analysis is important, but understanding the full picture is critical to implementing Principle Two—driving the share price by managing the customer portfolio. Despite the logic, some operating managers still kick up a fuss over allocating costs fully. We've found an effective way to reply. "Okay," we say, "there are operating costs and invested capital you think shouldn't be assigned to you or any other manager. In that case we'll just have to raise the capital-cost hurdle you have to clear in order to meet your objectives and earn your bonus. After all, the company as a whole has to make an economic profit after paying all its costs and accounting for all its capital, and for that to happen you'll have to contribute in a big way. So while the company has an overall capital cost of, say, 10 percent, we're going to consider it 25 percent for your division. If you can't earn more than that return on your invested capital, you're failing." Then we wait for them to scream. They eventually get the point.

The Growth Illusion: The Time Line of Customer Profitability

Understanding the truth about customer profitability can help a company avoid trouble it might otherwise walk right into, blissfully ignorant of what's about to go wrong. The danger is nowhere worse than in a seemingly fast-growing company. We've described the following scenario, which we call the growth illusion, to CFOs and CEOs of a number of companies, and their responses generally combine fascination with fear. A company is rapidly growing earnings per share but actually destroying shareowner value. They realize this could be happening at their own companies—and because of the way they measure and manage their businesses, ignoring customer profitability, they wouldn't know it. Stick with us through the numbers, because the result is eye-opening.

Imagine a company that launches a big push for new customers and manages to acquire 5,000 of them at a cost of $1,000 each. That amount is what the company spends on advertising, promotion, sales calls, and such to get those customers in the door; typically the company might spend $100 reaching each prospect and succeed with just one in ten. To keep things simple we'll assume that the new customers don't produce any business in the year in which they're acquired, so the company's operating profit in that year is $5 million lower than it otherwise would have been. That is, it has spent $5 million in the hope of realizing much more than $5 million in future profits.

Suppose this company typically holds its customers for three years, and it earns a fully loaded, properly calculated economic profit of $300 per year from each customer. Obviously the company is losing money; it's earning $900 on customers that cost $1,000 to acquire, and that's not even discounting the future earnings to reflect the time value of money.[1]

Yet, remarkable as it may seem, the company's investors and even its managers, looking at conventional operating results rather than at customer profitability, might not know for years that anything is wrong. Why not? Suppose that in its second year the company acquires just 1,000 more customers, again at a cost of $1,000 each, or $1 million. Since the 5,000 recently acquired customers bring in a profit of $300 each for a total of $1.5 million, the company shows a profit increase of $500,000. That's a nice change from the previous-year decline and the beginning of a good-looking trend line. It gets better. Suppose that in the next year the company again acquires 1,000 new customers for $1 million. Now it has 7,000 new customers bringing in profits ($1.8 million total) and shows a profit increase of $300,000 over the previous year. Repeat the pattern once more and profits again rise $300,000 over the previous year.

This company looks like a star. Investors are frantic to buy the stock. The directors are paying management zillions. Yet from a rigorous analysis of customer profitability we know that *every new customer is unequivocally destroying shareowner value.* The more customers the company adds, the more value it destroys.

Obviously this situation can't last forever. The chickens will eventually come home to roost—though they may take their time, depending on the dynamics of the business. In our example, the chickens arrive the following year. The 5,000 customers acquired in the big campaign, having stayed for three years, leave; if the company keeps adding 1,000 customers a year, and the cost and profit characteristics remain unchanged, the company suddenly falls into a steady state of losing $100,000 a year (that is, 3,000 customers bringing in $300 each, or $900,000, versus the $1 million acquisition cost of bringing in each year's new 1,000 customers). The stock collapses, top management gets fired, and everyone in the business world is marveling at how a company could go into the tank so fast.

Does this scenario sound familiar? Leaving aside the simplified numbers in the illustration, does it suggest perhaps Gap's experience as it furiously acquired new customers by opening new stores on every corner, then saw its stock collapse? Or WorldCom's spectacular run-up as it offered cash incentives to attract new customers, then crashed and burned? Or cellular phone companies nationwide that did the same thing?

The scenario seems to describe almost perfectly the experience of several enterprise software firms (such as Oracle, PeopleSoft, SAP, Siebel). When they acquire a new customer, the customer typically pays a big up-front fee (let's say $1 million) for the software and then an annual service fee (let's say $100,000 a year) for a certain number of years thereafter. The problem many of these firms encountered is that the lifetime income stream from the customers just wasn't enough to cover all the associated costs. But as long as the company was out there acquiring plenty of new customers every year, each one paying a $1 million up-front fee, the company could appear to be prospering—even though a proper customer-profitability analysis would have shown that it wasn't.

Joe Liemandt, founder and CEO of Trilogy, a privately held software company that uses a different business model, saw his competitors get into trouble this way. "If you have a revenue model like this and you want to grow your company, what do you do?" he asks. "You sell a couple of deals—more of them this year if you want to keep the growth rate. The year after that? You have to sell even more customers. Wait—next year? Even more new customers. Eventually you'll run out of customers, and that's when every enterprise software company falls off a cliff." They went over the cliff most recently when the economy slowed down in 2001 and signing up new customers became a whole lot tougher. The true economics of the business started to become apparent, and the profits and share prices of these companies crashed.

We hasten to add that we don't know for sure how precisely the scenario we describe is what afflicted these companies—and we suspect they don't know either. The circumstances are certainly suggestive. But what scares so many of the managers we talk to is that they have no idea whether they're facing this disaster because they don't know how to look across their firm's products, regions, and sales channels to understand customer profitability. They don't know what it costs them to acquire customers or how long they hold customers or what it costs to maintain them, so they have no idea how much money they make (or lose) on each one. Perhaps most troubling, these managers have little idea what they could do with such information even if it fell from the sky—and even if they did, their product-, territory-, or function-based organizational structure would stop them from doing it.

In light of these facts, you can't help wondering about some of the seemingly terrific growth stories that stock analysts and the financial media are continually hyping. Which are the real deal, and which are headed for flameouts? Data on customer profitability would help boards, managers, and investors enormously in answering that critical question.

The Illusion of Customer Profitability Averages

One of the most important actionable insights at any company is knowing not just the average level of customer profitability but also which customers are profitable or unprofitable, by how much, and why. We've observed that a company's average level of customer profitability can give some high-level insights, as in the AT&T Wireless case, but we've also cautioned that acting on an average number may cause more harm than good. The reason is what we call the illusion of averages.

In our growth illustration above we assumed for simplicity that all customers were economically the same; in reality that's never the case. The profitability of customers within a company often varies radically. For example, at Toronto-based Royal Bank—more advanced in its understanding of customer profitability than almost any other company we know—they've found that just 17 percent of customers account for 93 percent of the bank's profits. At other companies the disparities are even more extreme. A major software maker found that of its 307 customers, only 7 were profitable. A major media company we've worked with found that of its 1,017 advertisers, just 17 accounted for all the company's profit. Canada's Hudson's Bay Company found that at one of its retail franchises the top 30 percent of customers account for 325 percent of profits.

To understand the importance of the distribution of customer profitability, consider two struggling companies, A and B, each failing to earn its cost of capital. The economic profitability of the average customer at each company is the same, minus $15. But that average figure masks critically important differences.

Suppose that at company A, every customer is yielding this same dismal economic profit of minus $15. But at company B, half the customers are generating economic profit of $80 each, while the other half are yielding economic profit of minus $110 each, combining to create the minus $15 average. While the averages for A and B are the same, the implications are vastly different. Company A can't earn an economic profit with any customers and thus faces a bleak future. Company B, by contrast, is tremendously successful with half its customers and performing disastrously with the other half. If company B's managers can figure out which customers are in which group and why, and then focus on adding more great customers and doing more business with them, while converting or losing the terribly unprofitable customers, they have a great story for investors and the foundation of a premium P/E company. This type of customer *deaveraging* represents a powerful new way for companies such as B to reallocate resources in ways that will turbo-charge their share prices and create sustained premium P/E multiples. It can also lead to developing new products and eliminating others, expanding trade areas, and acquiring new skills to meet the needs of existing and new profitable customers.

This hypothetical example is more typical than most managers think. Extreme customer profitability distributions are common. Everyone in business talks about the Eighty–Twenty Rule—the observation that 80 percent of your sales often come from 20 percent of your customers, that 80 percent of your problems come from 20 percent of your factories, that 80 percent of your time is spent on 20 percent of your problems. When it comes to customer profitability, the inequality is often even more extreme. We've observed what we call the 150–20 rule: 150 percent of your economic profit comes from 20 percent of your customers. At the same time, the bottom 20 percent may actually lose money equal to 150 percent of profit, with the middle 60 percent of customers making up the difference, often yielding anemic levels of overall economic profit.

In light of the facts about customer profitability, it's clear why treating all customers as average in, say, a customer-retention or -acquisition program, could be a terrible way to try to make a company more valuable. We can see why treating different customers differently is key to creating and sustaining superior share price performance from customer knowledge.

The Huge Differences in Customer Profitability

Principle Two says we must drive the company's stock by managing the pieces of the customer portfolio. As we'll see in later chapters, these pieces are most naturally thought of as customer segments. It's obvious you can't manage customer segment shareowner value without being able to figure customer segment profitability. But what many companies find when they calculate the economic profitability of their customer segments is not at all obvious. They often find that some customers—the number may be surprisingly large—are not economically profitable. That is, simply by continuing to do business with these customers, the company is destroying shareowner value. If the company were to cut off these customers today, the company's value would go up (though as we've said, there's often a better alternative than walking away from an unprofitable customer).

You'll recall that Eva earned an economic profit of $250 a year for Multimax, and she was an average customer. Based on our experience and that of others, the actual distribution of customer profitability at

Multimax could well look like that shown in this chart. Each bar represents a decile of customers—that is, each bar represents 100,000 of Multimax's 1 million customers. But while the number of customers in each decile is the same, the profits the company earns from each decile varies enormously.

That average profitability figure of $250 per customer masks a huge disparity. A full 30 percent of the customers—deciles 8, 9, and 10—are reducing the value of Multimax because they earn a negative economic profit. Eva, the average customer, is in decile 5. Note that 40 percent of the customers—deciles 1 through 4—earn above-average profits, and the top 20 percent of the customers—deciles 1 and 2—actually account for about 150 percent of the profits!* These are truly angel customers.

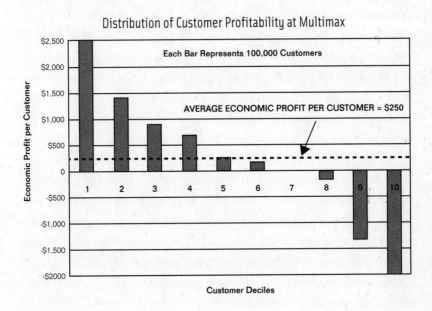

Distribution of Customer Profitability at Multimax

*That is, ($250 million + $150 million) / $250 million.

Disparities like this carry an extremely important implication. Research on customer loyalty has led to a rule of thumb, which has become conventional business wisdom, that increasing customer loyalty by 5 percent increases profits by 50 percent—or, depending on whom you're listening to, by 70 percent or 90 percent. But in a company whose customer deciles generate widely varying profits—meaning virtually all companies—it ain't necessarily so. For Multimax, increasing the loyalty of customers in the tenth decile of profitability could sharply *reduce* the chance of creating or sustaining a premium P/E; if Multimax didn't know which customers were in which deciles, it could easily commit resources to such a destructive program.

The fact that many customer deciles are unprofitable shouldn't be surprising. If costs, including capital costs, were strictly proportional to revenues, then maybe all customers could be profitable, but that's not reality. Besides the profits or losses from the product bundles each customer buys, every customer entails certain fixed costs, as well as some varying customer-specific costs—such as staff attention or customer maintenance costs—which may have little to do with revenue. For example, Europe's largest mutual life insurance company, Standard Life Assurance, ran a direct-mail marketing campaign that appeared to be successful; revenues rose. But then it analyzed the profitability of its new customers and found it had targeted the least profitable segment: elderly couples and stay-at-home moms who were glad to arrange lengthy—and extremely expensive—home visits by sales agents, and who then tended to buy small, single policies.[3] Far from a success, the campaign probably reduced shareowner value. By contrast, if a company can aim its acquisition and retention efforts just at customers in the top deciles, profitability should rocket.

And then there's the cost many companies overlook, the capital charge. In the chart above, we showed the *economic* profits of Multimax's customers. It's worth repeating that calculating customer profitability on this basis—that is, with an appropriate charge for capital—is essential, because only economic profit tells whether a company is creating or destroying shareowner value. The effect can be dramatic. A major printing company calculated customer profitability on a conventional basis—that is, ignoring the capital charge—and found that its largest customers appeared to be its most profitable. But it then recalculated on the basis of economic profit—that is, including an appropriate capital charge—and found just the opposite: Its biggest customers were actually highly unprofitable. The reason is that these customers required the company to hold large inventories of expensive specialty papers, which tied up lots of capital, and the charge for all that capital wiped out the apparent profits. By contrast, small customers the company served on an opportunistic basis, which it had thought were not very important, actually accounted for a significant portion of the company's economic profit.

Wasting money on efforts to attract and retain unprofitable customers does more harm than may first be apparent. How many highly profitable customers are leaving your company because they're getting an unsatisfactory experience—undifferentiated service, nonrecognition by salespeople, lack of appreciation for their changing needs—as a result of resources being squandered on unprofitable customers? It stands to reason that without spending one more dollar per customer, just shifting resources from unprofitable (low potential value) customers to profitable customers will produce staggering results for customers and shareowners.

Logical next question: To manage my own company in a way that uses these ideas, exactly what should I measure, and how? Those are the issues we tackle next.

$\triangle$ 4 $\triangledown$

Managing Customer Profitability the Right Way

What Your Real Goal Is and
a Practical Scorecard to
Track Progress

By now we've achieved a pretty good understanding of just how revealing customer profitability can be. We can also see quite specifically how the primary focus of the typical company—the products and services it sells, or the places where it sells them, or the functions that produce and deliver the products and services—can lead to trouble. That trouble can come in the form of not knowing which customers to invest in and which ones not to. Not knowing which customers are most profitable and have the greatest potential means not being able to identify their specific needs; this often leads to a massive misallocation of resources across customers, the products and services they need, sales channels such as stores, branches, or account managers, and the functions that have to deliver on customers' (especially angel customers') needs. But while customer-centered companies are clearly best positioned to create shareowner value by understanding customers' needs, any company intending to go down this road needs a more precisely defined goal than simply "more economic profit is better." The reason is that creating steadily more economic profit, difficult as that is, isn't enough. Every company is competing with every other company for the lifeblood of business, capital. To be sure of access to that critical resource on the most favorable terms, a company must be more than just good at creating economic profit on a sustained basis; it must be *better* than most other companies.

How can managers know, day by day, whether their company is winning or losing the competition to create superior value? Remember that in our rate-your-readiness quiz in Chapter 1, the first criterion was: Your leadership is committed to delivering and maintaining a premium P/E multiple.

In this chapter we'll explain exactly why a sustained premium P/E multiple is the best real-world, practical measure of management's performance. Then we'll show how managers can know whether the profitability of specific customers or customer segments is contributing to or detracting from a premium P/E for the company. And we'll introduce a new tool, the Customer Segment Value Creation Scorecard, that companies are using to show managers how they can measure and manage customer profitability so they'll know every day what actions they can take to push their company toward a premium P/E they can sustain.

Your Real Goal: A Premium P/E

To understand why a premium P/E is particularly significant, let's look at a dozen companies that over the five years from September 1996 to September 2001 were so far ahead of the pack they clearly won the battle for competitive dominance:

Dynamite Dozen

- ∀ Automatic Data Processing
- ∀ Bed Bath & Beyond
- ∀ Dell Computer
- ∀ General Electric
- ∀ Home Depot
- ∀ Kohl's
- ∀ Medtronic
- ∀ Microsoft
- ∀ Pfizer
- ∀ Starbucks
- ∀ Walgreen
- ∀ Wal-Mart

These Dynamite Dozen are widely recognized as stars. You won't be surprised to learn that on average their total return to shareowners[1] over the five years from September 1996 to September 2001, a period encompassing a raging bull market and a dismal bear market, was magnificent—more than double the average of the S&P 500. They also had roughly double the average revenue growth, profit growth, and return on capital.

Most of these companies deal with customers directly, not through intermediaries. That means they're in excellent positions to gather extensive customer data and to interact with customers in many ways. Some, such as Dell, are world-class in the sophistication of their customer data collection. Most of these companies, in stark contrast to the Dismal Dozen we met in Chapter 1, delight their customers every day. Some, such as Bed Bath & Beyond, Medtronic, Wal-Mart, and Starbucks, are famous for corporate cultures that utterly honor the customer.

In addition, these companies share another, highly significant characteristic that is apparent in the following chart:

DYNAMITE DOZEN: PREMIUM PERFORMANCE
5-Year Relative P/Es

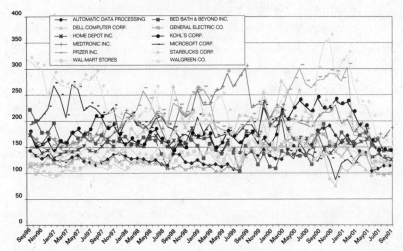

The bold horizontal line represents the average P/E multiple of the S&P 500 over that 60-month period. As you can see, all of these Dynamite Dozen maintained relative P/Es (i.e., company P/E divided by S&P P/E) above the average virtually all the time—a truly remarkable record.[2] These are the opposites of and the role models for the Dismal Dozen. If the Dismal Dozen could perform as well as the Dynamite Dozen, they would create more than $1 trillion of new shareowner value.

The fact that all of these excellent companies have maintained above average P/Es holds more meaning than may be apparent at first. It turns out that a company's relative P/E embodies a great deal of valuable information about shareowner value creation. And before the finance experts object that the *E* in P/E, earnings, is subject to all manner of distortions, let us note that we're well aware of that issue.

While it's a valid point, the fact is these companies achieved top-tier performance virtually every month for sixty consecutive months, an accomplishment that effectively filters out a great deal of potential noise in earnings. For now we want to focus on the concept.

A premium P/E is simply one that's higher than the overall market's average multiple—above the 100 percent line in the chart. The capital markets in which your company's stock and bonds get traded are in reality a competition that never stops. Every company out there wants to attract investors' capital by providing a more profitable home for it than your company does. A very useful and reliable sign of whether you're winning or losing this contest is your P/E relative to the market on a sustained basis: Is it better or worse than the average?

Here we see an attractive feature of the P/E multiple as a performance measure for managers. Markets go up and down over time, taking every company's multiple along for the ride. But no matter where you are in the hills and valleys, you can always compare your company's multiple with the average for the overall market and see where you stand. For example, General Electric, one of the Dynamite Dozen, had a P/E multiple of 44 in early 2000, at the bull market's height, but a multiple of only 36 a year later. A sharp drop in performance? Not really. Since the market's average multiple had declined from 32 to 25 in that time, GE was still doing far better than most companies, beating the average by an impressive margin. By contrast, Alcoa increased its multiple from 23 in early 2001 to 33 a year later—but hold the applause. Because the market's average P/E increased from 25 to 40 in that period, Alcoa was still a subpar performer.

A postscript on the Dynamite Dozen: Over the 16 months following the end of our five-year analysis period in September 2001, several companies, such as General Electric and Home Depot, dropped out of this elite group. New companies, such as Harley-Davidson and Johnson & Johnson, replaced the old stars as consistent five-year outperformers. The shuffling of players shows that, as in any global competition, remaining among the world's best for more than five years is extremely challenging.

Note that we want you to compare your multiple with the overall market's average multiple, not with your industry's or any other sub-group's. Managers in companies with lousy multiples often hide behind the rationalization that although their P/E is low, it's higher than the average for the industry. Automakers and investment banks are prime examples. It's not really their fault, they insist—"We're just in a tough business."

Sorry, guys, that won't do. The world's capital doesn't care what industry you're in. Investors are looking at all possible homes for their capital, in every industry, and if your P/E isn't beating the whole market's average, then you're losing the competition to be the most attractive place to park money. In reality, even a tough industry is no excuse. Southwest Airlines and Dell Computer, in two of the world's lowest-margin, most brutally competitive industries, have consistently achieved premium or at least par P/Es. Indeed, one of the best reasons to focus on achieving a premium P/E is that for many companies it's a stretch goal.[3] It sets the bar so high that managers are forced to abandon incremental thinking and instead must reinvent their relationship with customers.

Your P/E Is Your Future

A different perspective shows yet another reason we believe that achieving a sustained premium P/E should be your goal. One of the P/E ratio's most important traits, overlooked by many managers, is this: It embodies the market's judgment of your company's *future*—its performance for years to come.

In the formulas that finance specialists have developed to show what determines a P/E, there are two elements. One, the so-called nongrowth element, shows how much of the P/E comes from the company's performance today. If a company looked as if it would perform exactly as it did last year, every year into the future, this nongrowth element would constitute its entire P/E. Rarely is it more than 10.

The other element, the growth element, reflects the market's expectations for the company's profitable future investment opportunities. That's where the rest of the multiple has to come from, and obviously it's where nearly all the opportunity lies. If you want a premium P/E multiple—30 or 40 in today's market (with the S&P multiple in the low- to mid-20s)—your company will have to give investors good reason to expect spectacular performance in the future. And as we will stress repeatedly, profitable customers, present and future, are the ultimate source of this performance.

To see how dramatically these investor expectations can affect a firm's stock price and P/E multiple, consider two companies: Kohl's Stores, the fast-growing specialty department store chain and one of our Dynamite Dozen, and Tommy Hilfiger, which makes some of the apparel that Kohl's sells. As it happens, their earnings in the most recent twelve months as we wrote this were in the same neighborhood: $1.28 a share for Kohl's, and $1.47 a share for Hilfiger. Investors apparently think Hilfiger will just keep earning about $1.47 a share on average every year for as long as they can see. We know this because Hilfiger stock was trading at about $14 a share, for a subpar multiple of 9.5 (i.e., a relative P/E of less than 50 percent of the S&P). This P/E multiple thus consists only of the nongrowth element; there's no growth element at all. But investors think Kohl's will increase its profitability by big jumps every year, year after year. Its stock was selling for about $68 a share, for a big premium P/E multiple of 53 (a big relative P/E of over 200 percent). Since we know the nongrowth element can account for only about 10 in that multiple, the remainder—43—must be based on expectations of future growth.

Two companies with about the same profits, yet one has a stock trading for *five times* as much as the other. That's nice in more ways than one. For Kohl's, it triggers all those benefits for the company—helping it attract employees, fund projects, reinvest in strengthening its customer value propositions, and make acquisitions—that we discussed in Chapter 1. It also means that if Kohl's can increase next year's profit by just a little more than the market expects, that increase will get multiplied by 53 (Kohl's P/E multiple) before it's added to the stock price, as long as investors believe the increase represents a sustainable advance in the company's ability to earn. In fact, it might get multiplied by more than 53 if investors think the profit increase is a sign that the company has even better new investment opportunities than were expected—that is, if they decide the growth element in Kohl's P/E is greater than they had estimated.

Of course the wondrous effects of rising profits work just as powerfully in reverse, and it's not a pretty sight. If a company reports profits that are lower than expected, investors may conclude that big trouble is afoot and the company's future investment plans may be overambitious. In that case lower profits will result in a sharply lower price and may also result in a sharply lower P/E multiple. So if Kohl's earnings fall short of the market's expectations, that shortfall will get multiplied by 53 when it's translated into the share price. If investors think the stumble signals that Kohl's will now be growing at a slower rate long-term, the shortfall could be reflected in an even greater decline. This reverse multiplier effect is why we sometimes see companies lose 30 percent, 50 percent, even 70 percent of their value in one day. It doesn't happen just to start-ups or dot-coms, either. In the past few years we've seen it happen to Procter & Gamble (30 percent of total value lost in one day), Home Depot (20 percent), Oxford Health Plans (68 percent), and American Greetings (31 percent), among others.

Your company's P/E multiple thus summarizes in a single number the market's consensus view of your company's future, which makes it a remarkably useful indicator. It's an external, objective assessment determined by people and institutions placing their own capital.

Whether you think it's right or wrong, you had better compare your investor's assessment with your own internal view on the size of profitable future investment opportunities. How will you be using your owners' capital? As their expectations and your own change over time, your goal of a premium P/E remains constant through the ups and downs of the market and of your particular industry.

What Moves Your P/E

Ultimately just four factors determine whether you will have a premium, par, or discount P/E. They will determine whether the growth element of your P/E is large, moderate, zero, or actually negative. Managers should remember that these are the *only* factors that drive your P/E. This is a crucial point: Anything a manager does to fulfill his or her primary responsibility of increasing the share price and the P/E must come down to affecting one of these four factors. They are it! If you aren't moving at least one of these factors in a positive way, you may as well go take a nap; you'll be doing just as much to get the stock up, and maybe you'll have some creative ideas when you wake up. In fact, if you're not improving at least one of these factors, you're probably taking actions that are harming them, driving your stock and your P/E down. The nap sounds like an even better idea.

Here are the four factors and how they affect P/E:

1. and 2. Return on invested capital and **capital cost,** together with the difference between them, called spread, measure the true profitability of future investment opportunities. Since your P/E is entirely a reflection of your company's prospects, investors' expectations for your spread are key. As we've noted, the Dynamite Dozen had returns on invested capital about double the S&P 500 average. Those returns were almost double these companies' average cost of capital, resulting in huge spreads. No wonder these companies sustained premium

P/Es. Since investors don't have access to future expected spreads, they need proxies. Today's numbers often play a key role in forecasting tomorrow's, so your company's current and planned spreads are powerful factors in influencing your P/E.

3. Investment is a particularly strong factor in pushing your company's P/E up or down. It's simply the amount of money your company invests back into its business in excess of depreciation and amortization each year. The nongrowth component of your company's value and P/E requires that you invest back into the business at least enough to maintain the business's assets. The investment in excess of depreciation fuels the growth element of your P/E. A convenient way to express incremental new investment size—that is, investment beyond what's needed to cover depreciation—is as a proportion of the company's earnings. Of course the percentage can be over 100 percent if the company raises new capital to put into highly promising investment opportunities. Members of the Dynamite Dozen, such as Kohl's and Medtronic, have a history of very high levels of investment back into their businesses.

4. Duration also exerts a powerful influence on your company's P/E. This is the length of time your company can maintain returns on new investment in excess of capital cost. If investors have previously been unwilling to bet your company can maintain its positive spread for more than five years, and you persuade them you can actually maintain it for ten, our analysis suggests your P/E could increase 50 percent, enough to hurtle you from the back of the pack to the front in the race for investors' capital. Beware of going the other way. Investors' anticipated duration at Toys R Us probably plummeted after Wal-Mart started to get traction in the toy business some years ago, which is undoubtedly one reason its share price and P/E multiple also plunged.

A company can arrive at any given P/E through many different combinations of the four factors we've discussed: return on invested capital, capital cost, investment, and duration. But in practice, companies with premium P/Es tend to cluster in a sweet spot that looks like this:

Premium P/E Sweet Spot
- ⋎ return on invested capital > 25%
- ⋎ capital cost < 12%
- ⋎ investment (in excess of depreciation) > 70% of earnings
- ⋎ spread duration > ten years

Getting to this sweet spot isn't easy—only a small fraction of companies are able to do it. They're the companies that consistently achieve a P/E multiple that's 20 percent to 50 percent above the S&P 500 average, the winners in the unending competition to attract capital, the ones that will best be able to serve customers, employees, and shareowners. They're also the companies that dominate their industries, which is the group you want to join or remain in.

Intuitively, it's clear that if a company's capital costs are higher than 12 percent because of higher-than-average volatility of its business, then to realize a premium P/E the company's return on invested capital will have to be correspondingly greater. If the duration can be stretched out from ten to 12 years due to a totally dominant customer value proposition, then more of the company's profits can be reinvested in the customer, lowering its return on invested capital a bit while still sustaining a premium P/E.[4]

If you currently have a premium P/E and have been able to sustain it for a while, then no doubt you're meeting or exceeding the sweet spot rules of thumb. The question for you is whether your strategic plan will insure that you continue meeting or exceeding them. If not, you need to get to work before investors recognize that your returns on invested capital will fall, or new investment opportunities are becoming ever harder for you to find. For Wal-Mart, dramatically successful moves into toys and groceries were among the company's ways of meeting or exceeding the Street's expectations for investment. If you don't act, your stock is in grave danger of crashing.

If you are not in the fortunate position of having a premium P/E, but you are in fact hitting and have robust plans to continue hitting the sweet spot numbers, then your company faces a marketing problem: persuading investors that your prospects are much brighter than they think.

A New Tool: The Customer Segment Value Creation Scorecard

Operationally, the largest implication of accepting Principles One and Two—of seeing a company as a customer portfolio managed for shareowner value—is this: Now you need to know *how* each customer portfolio is contributing to or detracting from your company's P/E multiple, and not just in a general, qualitative way, but in hard numbers. Until you can figure that out, you can't implement this concept, which means you can't use it to achieve your bottom-line goal of creating shareowner value through realizing and sustaining a premium P/E.

We're now going to show you how to figure out exactly what you need to know. You have probably not seen an analysis like this before. Part of the reason is that for big companies, assembling the data on any large-scale basis was just too hard until recently, when computers and software made it possible. But the more important reason is simply that most companies haven't thought in these terms. Yet this is an analysis that any manager would like to see.

Some companies have recently begun performing related analyses to determine the lifetime value of a customer or segment, but even lifetime value is not, ultimately, what you most want to know. Most lifetime value calculations ignore capital costs, and since they're typically not grounded in the details of current customer profitability, they tell managers nothing about how to manage customers to increase the company's share price. What you want to know is whether a given customer or segment is creating or destroying shareowner value—specifically, whether it's helping or hurting your company's relative P/E, why, and what to do as a result.

We call this analytical tool the *Customer Segment Value Creation Scorecard*. Real companies are using their own versions of this tool today, and near the end of the chapter we'll show you examples of their Scorecards. First we want to explain the design of the Scorecard and what it tells.

In this example we're looking at a company with three customer portfolios or segments. For now we won't describe how a company identifies and defines its customer segments; that important subject is what Chapter 6 is all about. But the basic concept is simple and intuitive. Customer segments are groups of customers whose traits, needs, and desires are sufficiently similar that the members of the segment can be most profitably served with similar value propositions. So at Dell, for example, segments of business customers are defined by the size of the business and, in some cases, by their industry, such as health care or government. Customer segments are the most actionable way to form customer portfolios.

Within each segment we examine three groups of customers: current customers, new ones (that is, new since the last time the Scorecard was compiled), and lost customers. These groupings are important because they show us the customer-centered trends in our business. Are we gaining the kinds of customers we want to gain? Are our current customers responding to our value propositions in the way we want, or do we have to make changes? Are we losing valuable customers?

For each of these three groups, we classify what we sell (to current and new customers) or used to sell (to lost customers). The three categories of sales are products, services, and intellectual capital. We use

CUSTOMER SEGMENT VALUE CREATION SCORECARD

	Segment 1 — Products	Services	Int. Cap.	Total	Segment 2 — Products	Services	Int. Cap.	Total	Segment 3 — Products	Services	Int. Cap.	Total	TOTAL
Current													
Revenue													
Base Revenue	4,150	1,900	0	6,050	4,500	900	200	5,600	100	150	750	1,000	12,650
Up Sell													
Existing Products	200	50	0	250	500	0	0	500	10	0	50	60	810
New Products	200	0	0	200	500	0	0	500	0	0	50	50	750
Cross Sell													
Existing Products	0	0	0	0	100	0	0	100	0	0	0	0	0
New Products	0	0	0	0	200	0	0	200	10	0	150	160	210
New Customers	300	100	0	400	500	50	50	600	0	10	150	160	1,160
Lost Cust Revenue	-1,300	-200	0	-1,500	-2,300	-200	-50	-2,550	-20	-10	-50	-80	-4,130
Cust Winback Revenue	100	0	0	100	0	50	0	50	0	0	50	50	200
Total:	3,650	1,850	0	5,500	4,000	800	200	5,000	100	150	1,000	1,250	11,750
COGS	12.0%	18.0%	0.0%		8.0%	24.0%	45.0%		15.0%	25.0%	60.0%		
Account Management Costs													
Relationship Mgmt.								1,000				10	
New P/S/I Introduction													
New Account Costs													
Acquisition New Customers								500				32	
Win Back													
CKM Cost													
Product/Service Development													
Other Cost													
Nopat				550				250				250	1,050
Invested capital				3,929				2,500				500	6,929
ROIC				14.0%				10.0%				50.0%	15.2%
Capital cost				9.0%				10.0%				12.0%	9.7%
Economic Profit				196				0				190	386
Future													
ROIC				15.0%				8.0%				50.0%	14.4%
Investment %				65.0%				50.0%				125.0%	75.7%
Capital cost				9.0%				10.0%				12.0%	9.7%
Duration (yrs.)				11				10				13	11
P/E				16				9				60	14

these three categories because, as managers focused on shareowner value creation, we care passionately about return on invested capital, and this return varies dramatically across these categories. In general, products bring in the lowest returns because they normally can't be produced without physical assets (factories, machinery, inventories), all of which typically require substantial invested capital. Services generally yield higher returns on invested capital because they require less in the way of invested capital; a consultant or lawyer needs an office, a cell phone, and a laptop, and that's about it, yet his or her time can be billed at hundreds of dollars an hour. Intellectual capital frequently yields the highest returns on invested capital because it requires the least invested capital relative to the returns it brings in (unless the intellectual capital offering resulted from an expensive acquisition carrying lots of goodwill and other intangibles). Perhaps the best example is software: Once it has been created it can be reproduced at virtually zero cost, and it can be delivered over the Internet without ever assuming physical form at all. Some of the highest returns on invested capital in all of business are produced at software companies; at Oracle, for example, the figure was recently 54 percent. Because products, services, and intellectual capital can differ so dramatically in their returns, we want to know how much of each we're selling to whom.[5]

As you can see, we classify sales in another way as well. Part of the power of customer segment analysis is that we can see how well we're doing in selling customers not just what we've been selling them but also offerings they haven't bought before. On the Scorecard, we break out up-selling—that is, selling customers bigger, better, more valuable versions of what they're already buying—and cross-selling, which is selling them offerings from other categories. Within the up-sell and cross-sell sales figures, we break out how much came from new offerings created since the last Scorecard and how much came from previously existing offerings. All this information is necessary if we're to evaluate the success of the customer value propositions we are constantly creating, revising, and executing.

Combined, this information adds up to total revenue. Next we analyze costs—again, probably in ways you haven't seen before.

After recording the Cost of Goods Sold, a standard and familiar measure, we look at the costs of managing the customer accounts. These consist of the relationship management costs and the costs of introducing (as distinct from developing) new offerings. Next we examine the costs of bringing in customers who are new since the last Scorecard, distinguishing between customers we've never had before (acquisition of new customers) and those we once had, lost, and brought back (winbacks). These costs will seem unfamiliar in many organizations, but only because companies haven't been in the habit of compiling them. In a truly customer-centered enterprise (the kind that most companies claim to be) knowing these costs is absolutely essential.

The next category of costs can be explained only briefly for the moment. These are the costs of customer knowledge management (CKM on the scorecard), the costs associated with using customer knowledge to create, communicate, and support value propositions that are the engines for creating a premium P/E. (We explain value propositions in detail in Chapters 7 and 8.) We then break out the costs of developing new offerings and finally include a category for other costs that can't be classified into one of these categories. A number of revenue and cost elements are common across customer segments. Others are not, including those resulting from discounting or time spent serving customers. A combination of common sense and sophisticated tools, such as activity-based accounting, are essential in real-world applications.

Subtracting these costs as well as taxes from revenues gives net operating profit after tax—a familiar figure at last, though reached in a new way. If we then look at the total investment by category, we can easily figure out the return on invested capital for each customer segment. This is an extraordinarily valuable measure, one that often comes as a shock to managers who see it for the first time.

You will notice that the Scorecard has been divided into two parts, current and future. The latter incorporates estimates for the four factors driving a company's P/E. On the Scorecard these factors are estimated for each customer segment. Summing the projections across the segments gives a corporate total.

After forecasting each segment's return on invested capital, we can then estimate the percentage of each segment's operating profit that will be reinvested in that segment and the duration, the number of years the company can continue earning the current return from that segment. Estimating capital costs for each segment if there are significant differences in risk, we now have all the elements we need for calculating an *intrinsic* P/E for each customer segment. First for each segment and then for the company as a whole, we calculate a P/E ratio based on estimates of the four factors. The resulting P/E is based on what Warren Buffett sometimes calls an "intrinsic value," meaning a value determined by financial characteristics, as distinct from the conventional market P/E based on the market price of the company's stock at a point in time.

These figures are eye-openers. In the example, the company as a whole has a P/E of 14, which is below the overall S&P average of 22; that multiple of 14 is effectively a weighted average of the P/Es of all three customer segments. Segment No. 1 has a P/E of 16, better than the company's overall multiple but still not as high as the market's average multiple, so it's really not helping the company compete for capital. Segment No. 2 is a terrible performer, dragging down the corporate multiple with a P/E of only 9. And Segment No. 3, though small, turns out to be a star with an intrinsic P/E of 60.

Immediately we begin to see ways to create more shareowner value. We must figure out why two segments are underperforming and one is a star. Segment No. 1, which the company's managers thought was a solid performer, actually needs to be improved so it at least matches the market's average multiple; otherwise it's pulling the company back in the race for investors' interest. Segment No. 2 requires drastic action because right now it's killing the company. Can

Segment No. 3 be expanded fast, while maintaining its stellar multiple? Giving it more weight in the weighted average would obviously be a big boost to the company's P/E.

The Scorecard helps us understand all these issues. We have highlighted a few details to provide focus. How can Segment No. 1 be improved? Note that the company's sales to that segment are overwhelmingly products, which in general provide a low return on invested capital, and hardly any intellectual capital, with its generally fabulous returns. There's an opportunity. Note further that the company isn't up-selling *any* intellectual capital to Segment No. 1, nor has the company cross-sold any new offerings of any kind in Segment No. 1. These are big opportunities.

Look at the lost customers in Segment No. 1. It turns out they were far more likely to be buyers of intellectual capital than are the segment's average current customers. Winning them back and attracting more like them would be worth a lot.

As for Segment No. 2, that basket case, its problems are everywhere. It sells mainly products, and the products it sells yield a return on invested capital of just 8 percent, which is below its capital cost of 10 percent—so this part of the business is destroying shareowner value. A big reason for that low return is high costs; the segment's customers include a lot of particularly high-maintenance buyers whose relationship management costs are especially large at 20 percent of revenue. In addition, the company is spending a fortune attracting new customers into the segment (i.e., they're spending $500 to get $600 in new customer revenue). That's important because the segment is losing customers like crazy, and note that some of *those* customers were potentially value-creating: They might have been more likely to buy services than the segment's remaining customers. So managers can attack the Segment No. 2 problem on several fronts, though it's such a disaster that you've got to figure their first priority is probably getting much more knowledge and understanding of the segment.

It's obvious why Segment No. 3 is such a standout: Its customers buy almost exclusively intellectual capital, on which the returns are terrific, and it brings in lots of new customers at low cost. So if it's attracting all those new customers, why isn't it bigger? Because it's also losing too many customers. If the segment could substantially reduce that customer churn by investing more in relationship management given its excellent return on invested capital, it would be much larger while maintaining its excellent P/E, contributing significantly to improving the corporate multiple.

This example only begins to illustrate the ways in which the Scorecard can be used to understand and manage a company for a premium P/E. Here are some other ways to use the Scorecard as a competitive weapon to make your company more customer centered:

> ⅄   An initial version of the Scorecard can help the CEO and her senior team get the right questions on the table and create the right mind-set. Serving customers better and more efficiently becomes the unavoidable focus. The relative size of potential opportunities becomes clear, measured by current economic profit and growth potential.
>
> ⅄   The Scorecard can help break the traditional paradigms of managers retreating into defending their product, geographic, or functional silos because problems and opportunities are now defined primarily in terms of customers.
>
> ⅄   At the most senior levels of the organization, the Scorecard becomes the basis for planning and allocating resources, especially among customer segment business units. The sum of the individual customer segment plans becomes the corporate plan to be presented to the board. This overall plan needs to be tested against the overall corporate financial goals, such as realizing and sustaining a premium P/E, say within three years.
>
> ⅄   Scorecards for underperforming customer segments are

the basis for tough, fact-based fix-close-or-sell analyses, followed by swift decisions.

Ⅴ   The Scorecard can be used by customer segment managers to drive strategic planning and business reviews. By creating a target Scorecard, with an associated set of value propositions and actions to be taken, each segment leadership team can assess how they are or are not contributing to the corporate goal of a sustained premium P/E. This establishes a critical, explicit connection between customer segment value propositions and economic profit analysis, which is missing at most companies. It also becomes the first step in establishing accountability by customer segment managers for delivering on the economic profit plan.

Ⅴ   Creating a Scorecard for competitors forces a better understanding of competitors' economics and strategies. Aggregating competitors will produce an industry-wide Scorecard that will enable management to test its share of the total pool of economic profit.

Ⅴ   The Scorecard can be used at the level of sales and marketing management within customer segments to test alternative channels and sales coverage options. The focus is on retaining, growing, and acquiring customers with high economic profit and high potential.

Can you fill out the Scorecard for your company or unit today? In theory, the answer is always yes; the needed information is in your company somewhere, and with today's software tools you can find it, though you may never have even collected some of it. In practice, however, you may say the answer is no. The effort needed to extract the data would be just too great.

But why? In light of how critically important and enormously valuable this information is, why should getting at it be such an ordeal? The answer has little to do with technology. The problem is that most companies aren't organized in a way that makes anyone accountable for knowing this information, let alone accountable for acting on it. The product-, geography-, and function-based organizations in place at most companies offer zero incentive for any manager to take a company-wide, customer-centered point of view.

And by the way, if you can't fill out the Scorecard, how can you possibly say your company is customer-centered?

To illustrate how real-world companies are calculating the economic profitability of customers or segments today, consider the spreadsheet with which a television station owned by the New York Times Company, a pioneer among media companies in figuring economic profit, calculates the economic profitability of individual advertiser clients. As you can see, the managers analyze programming by type—news, local, network, syndicated—and time of day, and they look at differences in pricing, production costs, commissions, and sales effort.

Also nearby is the spreadsheet with which Royal Bank calculates the economic profitability of customer segments.

As a service business, Royal Bank needs to keep careful track of labor costs, which it does through a system of activity-based costing. By continually monitoring what it spends to serve customers through the bank's different channels, to process their transactions in the back office, to respond to them through the call center, and other activities, the bank can calculate its labor costs associated with any customer, based on that customer's bank products and transactions each month. The other information needed to calculate customer economic profitability—revenue, product spreads or invested capital—is relatively easy to assemble.[6]

For any company, the enormous power of this analysis is in what it enables managers to do. For the first time, they can see exactly where among their customers—the only source of revenue—the company is earning economic profit or loss, and then they can take actions they otherwise never would have known to take.

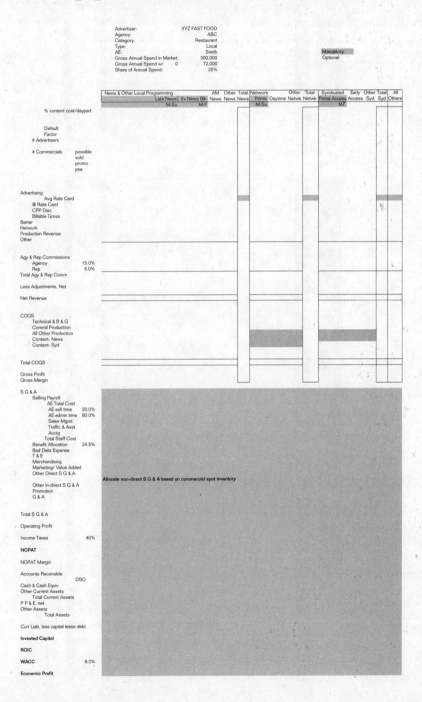

Advertiser:	XYZ FAST FOOD
Agency:	ABC
Category:	Restaurant
Type:	Local
AE:	Smith
Gross Annual Spend in Market:	300,000
Gross Annual Spend w/ 0	72,000
Share of Annual Spend:	25%

Mandatory
Optional

| | News & Other Local Programming | | | AM News | Other News | Total News | Network | | Other Netwk | Total Netwk | Syndicated | Early Access | Other Syd | Total Syd | All Others |
| | Late News M-Su | Ev News M-F | Blk | | | | Prime M-Su | Daytime | | | Prime Access M-F | | | | |

% content cost/daypart

Default
Factor
Advertisers

Commercials   possible
sold
promo
psa

Advertising
Avg Rate Card
@ Rate Card
CPP Disc
Billable Gross
Barter
Network
Production Revenue
Other

Agy & Rep Commissions
Agency   15.0%
Rep   5.0%
Total Agy & Rep Comm

Less Adjustments, Net

Net Revenue

COGS
Technical & B & G
Commil Production
All Other Production
Content- News
Content- Syd

Total COGS

Gross Profit
Gross Margin

S G & A
Selling Payroll
AE Total Cost
AE-sell time   20.0%
AE-admin time   80.0%
Sales Mgmt
Traffic & Asst
Acctg
Total Staff Cost
Benefit Allocation   24.5%
Bad Debt Expense
T & E
Merchandising
Marketing/ Value Added
Other Direct S G & A

Other In-direct S G & A
Promotion
G & A

Allocate non-direct S G & A based on commercial spot inventory

Total S G & A

Operating Profit

Income Taxes   40%

NOPAT

NOPAT Margin

Accounts Receivable
DSO
Cash & Cash Equiv
Other Current Assets
Total Current Assets
P P & E, net
Other Assets
Total Assets

Curr Liab, less capital lease debt

Invested Capital

ROIC

WACC   9.0%

Economic Profit

PERSONAL & COMMERCIAL

Personal & Business Products – Segment View – 2001 Full Year Actuals vs Full Year Plan

PRIME MARKETS

NOT SCORED

Income Statement	Key Market			Wealth Preservers			Prime Markets			Not Scored		
	FY Actuals	FY Plan	Var to Plan	FY Actuals	FY Plan	Var to Plan	FY Actuals	FY Plan	Var to Plan	FY Actuals	FY Plan	Var to Plan
	$M	$M	$M	$M	$M	$M	$M	$M	$M	$M	$M	$M
Mortgage Spread												
Loan Spread												
Deposit Spread												
Visa Spread												
Capital Spread												
Net Interest Income												
Other Income												
Gross Revenue												
NIE Mortgages												
NIE Loans												
NIE Deposits												
NIE Visa												
Total NIE												
Total PCL												
NIBT												
NIAT												
Economic Profit												
Financial Ratios	%	%	bps	%	%	bps	%	%	bps	%	%	bps
ROE												
Efficiency												
Balance Sheet	$MM	$MM	$MM	$MM	$MM	$MM	$MM	$MM	$MM	$MM	$MM	$MM
Average Res. Mtgs.												
Average Loans												
Average Deposits												
Average Visa												
Average Capital												

You're Now Miles Ahead of the Competition

It's worth stopping to think about what you know. You can determine, for any customer or customer segment, not only how much shareowner value is being created, but also an intrinsic P/E multiple that can be compared with the market's average multiple—thus showing whether that particular customer or segment is pushing the company toward its ultimate goal of a premium P/E or holding it back. This is an extraordinary thing to know. It enables managers to understand, far better than ever before, precisely how they are or are not achieving their most important goal, thus enabling them to manage to that goal more effectively.

Going a step further, you can now gain a *financial* understanding of any company not just in the traditional way as a collection of products, services, and geographic areas but also much more richly, usefully, and powerfully as a portfolio of customer segments, each with an intrinsic P/E. The company's own P/E is notionally the weighted average of these customer-segment P/Es.[7]

Any company wanting to improve its P/E must therefore examine its segment P/Es and act appropriately. Segments with low intrinsic P/Es need to be fixed, closed, or sold. Those with high intrinsic P/Es demand careful attention to the elements that create that high multiple; managers must protect the large spreads and long durations and must realize all profitable investment opportunities.

Before going further, let's pause to reflect on the big step we've taken. From this point forward, in keeping with Principle One, we propose to regard every business as a portfolio of customer segments. That is probably not how you currently regard your business or any other. It's a major conceptual change that will require some getting used to. As we shall see, it demands major organizational and cultural changes at most companies. Yet the reasons for it are overwhelmingly strong and get stronger as we examine the implications of this conceptual change more deeply. If, along the way, you sometimes find yourself asking, "Could someone tell me again why we're doing this?" just remember: Customers are where we must focus our efforts and must therefore be the foundation of how we understand and manage the company.

Experience tells us that at this point, having seen the power of deeply understanding the economic profitability of customers, you're beginning to realize some of the implications. These implications are so important that we'll spend most of the rest of the book discussing them. One of them bears mentioning here, immediately, because we've found that it's often the first one people must come to grips with.

When a company views itself as a portfolio of customer segments and completes its Customer Segment Value Creation Scorecard, the realization that some segments are more valuable than others, based on short-term economic profitability and future profitable growth opportunities, suddenly becomes blindingly obvious. Most managers have a vague understanding of this, but once we understand that some segments are increasing the company's P/E while others are pulling it down, we see immediately that *we can't treat these segments the same*. It's imperative that we keep and grow the most valuable segments, so we need to meet their needs better than average; the least valuable segments, which may actually be destroying shareowner value, must be treated differently, in a way that gets them generating positive economic profit—or, as a last resort, they can be shut down or sold.

It seems obvious, yet many companies run into big problems right here, at the very first action item. The problem is a deep cultural belief that all customers should be treated the same. In some companies this attitude grows out of a founder's proud egalitarianism: The little guy can come to our store and be treated just as well as anyone! In other companies it may be a residue of history. At phone companies and certain other regulated businesses, it was virtually illegal for years to treat different customers differently, though deregulation has since removed many of those restrictions.

It's an odd attitude. After all, as customers we expect to be treated better if we're big or loyal buyers, and many such customers get indignant if they aren't treated better. That fact is important to keep in mind when we move to the other side of the transaction. Many banks differ service only by a few broad segments, and they hesitate even to tell customers that better service is available in the next segment up, apparently from fear of offending those who don't qualify. But people clearly accept that better customers get better service, and today's technology lets companies identify better customers more easily and precisely than ever. It must become culturally okay to treat them better. Not doing so means misallocating scarce corporate resources away from customers that drive a company's stock and its futures. It means missing a giant opportunity to retain more customers, attract new customers, sell more to existing customers, and thus create value.

Failure to treat different segments differently is an even worse problem in a down economy. In reducing expenses, companies typically cut back everyone's service equally, for example, dropping head count in branches, call centers, and installation centers. Just when it's most essential to keep the most valuable customers and take more of their business away from competitors, these undifferentiated cost cutters are doing exactly the opposite. High-value customers leave. Meanwhile, low-value customers, who probably don't expect much, aren't disappointed and stick around in droves. The company's P/E is sure to drop faster than the market's.

At this point you're ready to take a first crack at the Customer Knowledge IQ Test. Using the concepts we've discussed, it reveals how well you really know your customers, and how well prepared your company is to manage itself as a portfolio of customers. Most companies find this test extremely challenging. But please regard it seriously, because it's a checklist of what you'll need to know about your own business before you can manage it as a portfolio of customers.

Understanding the concepts explained so far is a huge step toward delivering greater shareowner value through understanding customers more deeply, but it's only the first step. For virtually any existing company, managing the firm as a portfolio of customers is a matter of applying these concepts in the real world of organizational life. Doing so will probably require overcoming organizational and cultural obstacles. So let's turn now to how that gets done.

Customer Knowledge IQ Test

Part 1: For Business-to-Business Companies

1. Who are your "best" accounts?

    a. How do you define best?

    b. What is the economic profitability (in dollars) and return on invested capital (in percentages) of your best account?

    c. How do you set your profitability target for each account?

    d. Who are your worst accounts? What are their profitability levels?

    e. What is the minimum required profitability per account?

2. How do you define the level of your customer knowledge?

    a. How do your products and services affect your accounts' strategy?

    b. How do your products and services affect your accounts' revenue, assets, and income?

    c. How strong is the senior management relationship between your company and your accounts? CEO to CEO?

    d. Who are the real decision makers in each customer organization?

    e. What is your company's share of wallet (in dollars and percentages) with your accounts?

    f. Who are your major competitors? What are their killer value propositions?

    g. If you were to increase your prices by 10 percent, how many customers would you lose?

3. Do you segment your customers?

    a. What is your basis for customer segmentation—industry, geography, size, other?

b. How are you serving each segment differently from the others?

c. What profitability goals per segment do you set?

d. What are the benefits of serving segments differently—improved profitability? Something else?

4. How do you target new accounts?

a. Why do you target those accounts?

b. How will you serve each one of them differently from the others?

c. What will be the results of serving them differently?

d. How do you decide how much of your resources to invest in target segments?

5. What are your churn rates by customer segment?

a. What are the top reasons for the churn? How do you win back lost accounts?

b. Do segments constitute a certain concentration of products or services? Why?

6. Which accounts are in each decile by revenue and profitability?

a. What are the noticeable similarities and differences between customers in the different deciles?

b. What percentage of your accounts contribute 80 percent of your profitability? Of revenue?

7. What are your churn rates by decile?

a. What are the top reasons for churn in each decile? What do you do to win back lost accounts?

b. Do top deciles constitute a certain concentration of products or services? Why?

8. What can be done to increase your retention rate?

a. What are the differences in retention among profitability deciles?

b. Are the business units structured to retain profitable customers for a long time?

Part 2: For Business-to-Consumer Companies

1. Who are your best customer segments?

a. How do you define best?

b. What is the economic profitability (in dollars) and return on invested capital (in percentages) of your best customer segments?

c. How do you set profitability targets per customer segment?

d. Who are your worst customer segments? What are their profitability levels?

e. What is the minimum required profitability per customer segment?

2. How much do you know about your customers' or customer segments' purchasing behavior?

a. What is their frequency of visit?

b. What is their conversion rate?

c. What is their average spend per transaction?

d. What was their total spend with you during the past five years?

e. What is the size of their wallet? What percentage is spent with you?

f. Do they prefer your value propositions over your competitors', and if so, why?

g. If you were to increase your price by 10 percent, how many customers would you lose?

3. How are you segmenting your customers?

    a. What is your basis for customer segmentation—needs, lifestyle, geography, other?

    b. How are you serving each segment differently from others?

    c. What are the benefits of serving segments differently—improved profitability? Something else?

4. Which customer segments do you target?

    a. Why do you target those segments?

    b. How would you serve each segment differently from others?

    c. What would be the results of serving them differently?

    d. How do you decide how much of your resources to invest in target segments?

5. What is your customer or customer segment profitability?

    a. What is customers' or segments' frequency of transaction, transaction amount, longevity, recency, etc.?

    b. What do you do to affect customers' behavior? How do you monitor the changes?

    c. What are the differences in profitability between customers or segments?

△ 5 ▽

Organizing Around Customers

Why Do It and Why More
Companies Don't Do It

● ───────────────

"It was like going from capitalism to communism!" said Gail Mc-Govern, head of the Fidelity Personal Investments business at Fidelity Investments, the world's largest mutual fund company.[1] She was describing what happened when she reorganized her business from a traditional product- and function-centered model to one that is truly customer-centered—and in using the metaphor of capitalism and communism, she didn't mean she switched from free enterprise to central planning. Rather she was trying to convey the magnitude of the conceptual shift, the complete change in mind-set that every employee had to make. As her metaphor suggests, it wasn't a minor change. But it was emphatically worthwhile. As a result of it, Fidelity Personal Investments has achieved higher customer satisfaction, higher employee satisfaction, and the bottom-line payoff, higher economic profitability.

Why do we believe so passionately that your company should make this same dramatic shift and organize itself around customers?[2] We've already suggested why it makes sense from a *logical* point of view:

⩡ Customers are the only source of revenue and profits.

⩡ Knowing each customer's profitability or unprofitability, and the reasons for it, is critically important to creating winning value propositions that will drive your stock.

⩡ Understanding customers' different needs and behaviors is central to serving them most profitably.

⩡ Obtaining and analyzing this information used to be overwhelmingly difficult but now is practical.

⩡ Therefore, centering the company on customers is the way to go.

Armed with our knowledge of what creates economic profit and a premium P/E, we've seen additional powerful *financial* reasons for organizing the company around customers or customer segments, tying into the four factors driving a company's P/E:

⩡ Being customer-centered leads to higher *returns on invested capital* than being product-, territory-, or function-centric. This is especially true for product-centric companies that have sold few services. The reason is that customer-centered companies focus on meeting the customer's total needs, and this objective often leads the company to offer services and intellectual property, on which profit margins are almost always much higher than on products, and on which the return on invested capital is often obscenely high because so little invested capital is needed.

⩡ Being customer-centered leads to optimizing the portfolio of profitable versus unprofitable customers, again bringing in higher returns on invested capital. Focusing on products or geographies can lead to serious suboptimization, as we've already discussed.

⋎   The consistency of financial results that comes from those long, carefully managed customer relationships can produce lower *capital costs*. As you'll recall, the capital markets like consistent performance and offer capital to reliable performers on more attractive terms than to erratic performers. That translates into a lower cost of capital, which results in a higher economic profit. And higher economic profit—or, more precisely, the expectation of higher economic profit—is what makes share prices go up and leads to a premium P/E.

⋎   Being customer-centered creates opportunities to better understand customer needs and create superior value propositions, including a better managed customer relationship. This can result in much longer *durations* of positive returns in excess of capital costs. It is the strength of the value proposition that protects you from the inevitable onslaught of competitors, some of whom know only one game: price.

⋎   Because of their intimate understanding of customer finance and unmet needs, customer-centered companies will see larger *investment* opportunities than will companies organized in other ways.

These *logical* and *financial* advantages of organizing around customers, while extraordinarily powerful, are in fact secondary to an even more important, overwhelming *executional* advantage: Organizing around customers is simply the only way to make sure a business actually puts the customer at the center of its universe. Only by organizing around customers does a company have a prayer of understanding customer needs and behavior and collecting the right customer data in order to create, communicate, and reliably execute a superior value proposition, aimed at the right customers, that will increase shareowner value and lead to a premium P/E. Thus, organizational structure is a key competitive weapon.

Why It's All About Accountability

The all-important reason why organizing around customers is organizationally superior, as we have said before and will say again, is accountability. Everyone who has worked in an organization understands that nothing good will happen unless someone is accountable for making it happen. Specifically, with regard to customer data, it's relatively easy for everyone to agree that customer financial analysis is important. This is what consultants call a head-nodder: You point it out, and everyone nods. But following where it leads, making the changes that are always necessary in order to really drive a company's stock—these actions will meet resistance in an organization. Unless someone is accountable for using the analysis to produce measurable improvements in economic profitability, it almost certainly will not happen.

Think back to Chapter 1 and our story of the bank customer whose bank blew some great opportunities to get more of his business. As you'll recall, the bank had huge volumes of its own data about the customer, so it should have known he was a highly profitable customer with substantial long-term potential who deserved a special deal on a mortgage. The bank also had access to third-party data that would have revealed, or at least suggested strongly, his big relationships with other financial services firms, which the bank could have gone after. In short, the bank could easily have known everything it needed in order to create an offer that would have made this customer a highly profitable, delighted, long-term customer of the firm and a contributor to a higher share price.

Yet it didn't happen, and the reason is that no one was accountable for making it happen. It was no one's job to develop a plan, take action, and produce results based on everything the bank knew and could know about this customer or the thousands like him who yield hundreds of millions of dollars of profit for the bank. Instead, in this business as in most, the executives accountable for financial performance are those who run the various product, territory, and functional divisions. In this business as in most, it would be rare for any given customer to be highly profitable to every division, though a given customer could be highly profitable from the perspective of the bank overall—a perspective no customer-facing manager has. Thus, one executive is trying to maximize brokerage profits, another is trying to maximize mortgage profits, another is trying to maximize the branch networks' profits, and they do not have a clue that collectively they are actually driving the only source of profits—valuable customers—out the door. The dismal effect on the share price is only a matter of time.

Organizing around anything other than customers almost always results in misaligned incentives that produce crazy, value-destroying behavior. For example, when Fidelity Investments' Personal Investments business reorganized around customers in a rigorous way, specific executives became accountable for creating value for and realizing economic profit from customer segments. But before moving to this structure, the business was traditionally organized around functions—in this case, marketing, distribution, and systems and operations (with dotted-line connections to e-business). The marketing chief was evaluated on how much revenue he brought in. Whether the revenue resulted in profits wasn't his concern. He got paid for making the phone ring, so he was always pushing for more advertising.

But that was actually a problem for the distribution chief, who was in charge of customer service. She ran the big telephone service centers that are the heart of a mutual fund company; when the marketing chief made the phones ring, the service centers were where they rang. But the distribution chief, who was of course constrained by a budget, got evaluated on how quickly the phones got answered; her goal was to answer 85 percent of the calls within twenty seconds.

So she was incentivized to pray for the phones not to ring. And when the marketing chief made them ring anyway, the distribution chief could have cheated by having operators answer calls within twenty seconds and then put them on hold; that way she would satisfy her evaluation criteria, even though she was making some customers mad.

And the chief of systems and operations? He was in charge of risk and managing costs. In his continuing efforts to reduce risk, he would have to impose restrictions on margin trading, a profitable business for Fidelity. Changing rules caused problems for customers, and again made the phones ring. More problems for the distribution chief, who would end up being incentivized to argue against rule changes—not for the good of the customer or the good of the company, but to alleviate her own operational issues. Furthermore, the chief of systems and operations was incentivized to cut costs. He tried reducing head count in the back office—but what happened? Customers who used to be able to transfer securities between Fidelity and other brokers in two days found the time exploded to fifteen days. So what did those customers do? They called the service center.

Result: The business got along, in part because Fidelity has a strong tradition of offering extremely good customer service, and all the key players tried their best to do what was best for Fidelity and its customers. Yet even with a pro-customer culture, everyone in the organization knew that internal conflicts and misaligned incentives were preventing customers from being served optimally and preventing the company from creating maximum economic profit.

A Smarter Way to Allocate Scarce Resources

Every organization allocates resources. Whoever is accountable for the customer will not be able to create, communicate, or deliver the winning value proposition if he or she can't get appropriate resources. Allocating resources is one of the most fundamental problems in business;

innumerable books and articles have been written on its theory and practice. But most of this work never questions the implicit managerial assumption that scarce resources must be allocated among various product lines, functions, or territories; the only question is how to do it.

To organize a company around customers is to undermine this assumption and suggest that most managers have been asking the wrong question—which of course they have. They've been sweating bullets over how much money and people to give the lock-washer division versus the brake shoe division, not realizing they've been ticking off a highly profitable customer (who quietly buys brake shoes at list price but can't get them delivered exactly where and when he wants) while squandering resources on customers they don't realize are unprofitable because they buy loads of both products but demand deep price concessions and tons of special treatment. Instead, managers should be asking how best to allocate resources among customers and customer segments—which customers should get more resources, which less, and what kind of resources to each?

As we've seen, attempting to optimize resources across products almost guarantees that the customers who drive a company's share price over the long term won't get funded first. That funding may not be about products at all; maybe it's about customer care. For example, if an airline had a customer segment chief in charge of customers who fly first-class, do you think there would *ever* be a case of such a customer, who may be paying $5,000 or more for a ticket, not getting his first choice of meal? But in reality most airlines don't have such a customer segment chief. Instead they have an executive in charge of catering, whose job is to keep costs low—so these supremely profitable customers sometimes get ticked off because they can't get what they want to eat. It's insane.

Organizing around customers is a deeply different resource allocation mechanism. Because it uniquely assigns resources to the best opportunities from a company's ultimate source of revenue, profit, and shareowner value, it's a superior mechanism.

Organizational Structure Is a Competitive Weapon

Changing the form of organization is a big, even frightening step for most companies. But now we can see why it's worth taking. When organizing around customers, organizational structure actually becomes a competitive weapon. That is, the truly customer-centered enterprise can consistently take business away from any competitors organized around something else. It gathers more relevant customer data and uses it to create better value propositions than any competitor, because the managers creating them are focused on the customer's entire experience, not just on how to sell more of a product or service. Dell Computer and Royal Bank have outperformed competitors in exactly this way. The truly customer-centered enterprise executes value propositions better because managers are accountable for the total results of creating, communicating, and delivering them well, rather than being accountable for only the results of a particular dimension—the product, territory, or function. It allocates resources more effectively because it knows better than any competitor does where those resources can be applied to generate profit from the only source of profit: customers.

As a result, the high-performing customer-centered firm is a better financial machine than any competitor organized in a traditional fashion. It creates more economic profit, with all the advantages that brings: an ability to attract capital at lower cost, which in turn leads to even more economic profit; superior ability to attract the best employees, who want to participate in all this wealth creation and play a key role in providing superior execution of the customer value propositions; a more valuable currency—the stock with which to buy other firms. These factors combine to form a virtuous circle that just keeps making the firm stronger. As capital flows toward the customer-centered firm, competitors become starved for it and fall farther behind; as the best employees migrate to the firm, competitors have to make do with the second-best and have a harder time mounting a challenge; because investors reward the customer-centered firm with a more valuable stock, the firm can outbid competitors to buy other companies that have the products, services, technologies, or people that will enable it to serve customers better still; eventually it may even buy those competitors themselves, if they're still worth buying.

Organizational form can be more than a matter of competitive dominance. It can be a matter of survival. Question: If you're a retailer, how are you going to survive the onslaught of Wal-Mart? The Beast of Bentonville is not just the world's largest retailer, it's the world's largest company of any kind. To meet its relentless growth targets, it must increase revenues by some $40 billion every year—the equivalent of adding a Sears a year! To grow that much, Wal-Mart must continually expand into new areas of retailing. Who is America's biggest grocer? Kroger? Safeway? Albertson's? Not anymore. Who's America's biggest toy retailer—Toys "R" Us? Used to be, but no longer. Wal-Mart is continually expanding not just its scale but also its scope, meaning no retailer can ignore the threat it poses. But how can any retailer hope to withstand Wal-Mart? It has the best market intelligence, the best logistics, the greatest buying power.

One thing we know for sure is that no one will beat Wal-Mart by playing Wal-Mart's game. But it may be possible to survive Wal-Mart by playing an entirely different game—by being customer-centered. Indeed, we believe this strategy may hold the only realistic hope of survival for many retailers that stand squarely in Wal-Mart's path, such as Kohl's, Target, Costco, and in the United Kingdom, Tesco. Understanding the profitability of different customers and customer segments, formulating different value propositions for each, and executing those value propositions by driving them to the ledger every day—that is, being customer-centered—amounts to a superpowerful strategy for any retailer, and, crucially, it's a strategy Wal-Mart doesn't follow at all. It doesn't do any of those things.[3]

Wal-Mart is one of those companies we have discussed before that believes in its bones that all customers should be treated the same.

And that's fine—but as we have discussed elsewhere, there is always an opportunity to be found in customers who will respond to offers crafted just for them. That's a game at which Wal-Mart can't beat you because it's a game Wal-Mart doesn't play. Some of its competitors are realizing the opportunity. For example, one of Britain's most successful supermarket chains, Tesco, is up against ASDA, which Wal-Mart has bought and which is following Wal-Mart's strategy. Using a loyalty card program, Tesco collects data on the purchases of millions of its customers and then sends out customized quarterly mailings to each of them. The mailings are designed to increase customer profitability in various ways: by getting customers to shop more frequently, or by encouraging them to bundle profitable products with products they already like to buy, for example. Tesco says its customer data is its most valuable corporate asset.

A lesson that can be applied more generally is that Wal-Mart would actually have a difficult time becoming truly customer-centered. By now it has become so deeply invested in a strategy that doesn't differentiate among customers, it would face significant structural and cultural impediments to changing. For example, if it were to attempt customized promotions to individual customers, like Tesco, it would have to stock its stores differently. But it already has the world's largest system for stocking its stores for its undifferentiated model.

None of this means Wal-Mart couldn't become truly customer-centered if it wanted to. But this company, like many others with which you may compete, would face huge challenges, and that could be a great competitive opportunity for you. For some companies, becoming customer-centered—not just in attitude, but in organizational structure—is a competitive advantage that may be literally a life or death matter.

Different Ways to Organize Around Customers

What is organizing around customers? To understand how markedly it differs from traditional forms, consider first a typical organization chart. The chart below shows the function-centered organization of Fidelity Personal Investments in 1998 before the operation was reorganized around customers.

In moving past this form to some kind of customer-centered organization, most companies end up considering various options that range along a spectrum. At one end—the least committed and least successful—no manager has any significant accountability for the profitability of customers or customer segments, nor the resources or authority to drive such profitability. At the other end—the most committed and successful—specific managers have total accountability for

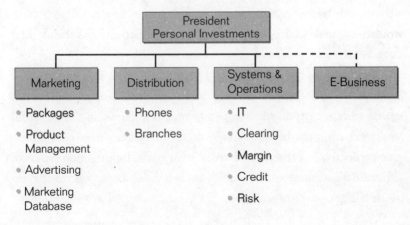

1998–Functional Structure

customer profitability; they're allocated resources on that basis and have the authority to realize the customer profit potential.

A commonly seen organizational form at the unsuccessful end of the spectrum is a loose matrix structure with informal lines of authority. Though often accompanied by platitudes about serving the customer, this is bogus customer-centricity—all hype but no real accountability or customer-based resource allocation. Some executives have cosmetic responsibilities that include an overall view of customers, while others are in charge of products or territories. Recall how heads of marketing and distribution at Fidelity were supposed to cooperate to serve the customer, but neither had a customer P&L. Instead, they were compensated on conflicting metrics. In general, managers at companies with this structure are supposed to consult with one another and work together to prevent problems like the ones in our bank example. But most often the product, territory, or function managers are ultimately accountable for profit and loss in their respective parochial domains, and that means their decisions will suboptimize the overall customer view, and they will repel all challenges to their fiefdoms. Authority and accountability are not aligned. If anyone but the CEO is charged with big-picture accountability for customers, then that person doesn't have the necessary authority and feels frustrated.

We know a major technology firm that is trying this loose matrix structure now. A new, high-level, customer-facing operation is supposed to represent all the company's products to its major industrial customers. But the heads of the product divisions—still the kings of the company, because they have P&L responsibility—don't like it. Their attitude, as one of the company's top executives summed it up to us: "Those are my customers." Those managers have the most organizational clout, and properly so; their necks are on the block when it comes to delivering product profits. So who will tell them that, for the overall benefit of the customer and the firm's economic profit, they can't do what they want to do? No one. This company was hoping to arrest a long decline in its stock, but it hasn't succeeded. It continues to lose ground to competitors.

Many companies, including several of the underperformers we described in Chapter 1, use an organizational structure like this today. Its appeal is that it seems least disruptive to the organization. But like most halfway measures, it offers no competitive advantages at all. As a practical matter no one is in charge of the customer, and little if any customer segmentation gets done, except perhaps in marketing. But no one will listen to marketing's recommendations. No one knows the reality of customer profitability because no one has any incentive to perform an analysis with fully loaded costs and invested capital. So no one can create value propositions that truly meet their most profitable customers' needs. For this reason, the fact that the organization would be utterly unable to deliver such value propositions is actually moot.

Moving farther along the spectrum is a kind of organizational structure sometimes called a hard matrix. There are formal customer managers as well as product or territory managers, and they are jointly accountable for P&L. This is a move toward accountability for the customer. Whether it works is largely a matter of the "soft" organizational factors—culture and leadership.

This is the structure used by Royal Bank, one of the most advanced customer-centered companies anywhere. The retail portion of the company has nine segment managers, each of whom has primary responsibility for strategy and the profit and loss of his or her segment. But the bank also retained its old product-centered organization; the customer-centered structure was simply placed on top of it. So the product managers still have responsibility for product profit and loss. In addition, managers in charge of functions (marketing, human resources, facilities management, and so on) compete for resources with the product and segment managers.

The idea was to encourage all these managers to collaborate, but of course it wouldn't necessarily work that way. It seems to work well at Royal Bank in part because the company's culture was always customer-centered, even if the organizational structure didn't optimally support that culture. The new organization in effect enabled employees to move the way they were already leaning. In addition, the bank has long had a culture of consensus rather than bitter internal competition, so a fair amount of the hoped-for collaboration actually happened. Segment managers do not have absolute authority to direct the product or functional managers and instead must rely on persuasiveness and teamwork skills to get things done. In the Royal Bank culture that's possible, though in certain other companies it wouldn't be. Another important factor in the success of this arrangement is the role of Jim Rager, the Royal Bank vice chairman in charge of retail operations, called RBC Banking. The reorganization was his initiative, and he made it clear that he wanted it to succeed. Failure to manage for the good of the team, and for the success of the reorganization, would not enhance one's career prospects.

Despite Royal Bank's success with the hard matrix structure, it carries a potential problem that almost always accompanies joint responsibility: No one will get full blame if things go wrong or full credit if they go right. So if the corporate culture and leadership aren't just right, it's always possible that no one will exert the effort and creativity needed to maximize the value of the company's current and potential customers.

All the way at the other end of the organizational spectrum is a structure in which customer segments are the primary P&L units of the company. They are the clear focus of accountability and the basis for resource allocation. The chart on page 105 shows Fidelity Personal Investments as it was structured in 1999, around customer segments.

All the company's customers are classified into one of several segments. A manager—a customer segment CEO—is in charge of each one, with full P&L responsibility. These segment CEOs are also fully responsible for segment strategy. Product and territory managers are explicitly subsidiary to the segment CEOs. Thus the company's operating profit is the sum of the segment profits.

This structure, at its best, gives the segment CEOs the needed incentive to create winning value propositions for their customers and create a premium P/E. These segment managers must understand customer profitability, incorporating all costs, including capital costs. They will—if they want to keep their jobs and earn big bonuses—do all the things we've talked about to make unprofitable customers profitable and make profitable customers more profitable.

This is the structure used by some highly successful customer-centered companies. At Fidelity, for example, the segment managers are accountable for the profit and loss of their segments, and they report directly to the president of the business. The company still has product managers, who are still extremely important, of course; but they are no longer where the bottom-line P&L resides. As one Fidelity

1999—Segmentation Structure

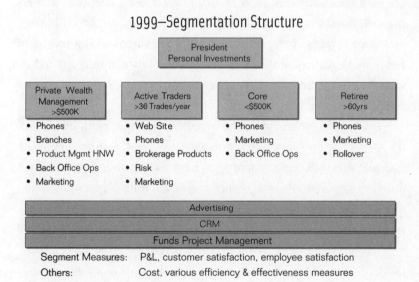

executive said to us, in a statement that sums up the change quite well, "Products are just vehicles for serving customers." An obvious statement, but a revolutionary perspective in most companies.

We've identified these points along the spectrum for illustration, but note that we're talking about a true spectrum, with an infinite number of points on it. Different companies have shown that they can succeed with different structures. That's why a universal form of organization is something we won't presume to prescribe in this book; every company is unique, and obviously we can't discuss every possible combination of traits. We can talk about the mechanics of incentives, and these are crucially important, but ultimately organizations aren't machines, they're human creations.

Note that as we move along this spectrum we encounter trade-offs. The low-accountability end of the spectrum may actually offer advantages in efficiency. Because there is no meaningful segmentation of customers, it may be possible for all the company's customers to use common functions, such as a call center. At a deeply customer-centered company like Fidelity, the phone calls of certain customers, identified through caller ID technology, are automatically routed to service reps with training in that customer's particular interests and issues. But in a company without segmentation, any rep can take any call, which is clearly a lower-cost approach.

Toward the other end of the organizational spectrum, but not all the way there, we encounter situations like RBC's (Royal Bank of Canada) in which segment managers have accountability yet still must use the corporation's staff functions—back office processes, sales, marketing—in common. This setup puts heavy demands on the corporate culture. All the way at the extreme of accountability, where each customer segment is operated as a virtual freestanding company, there may be sacrifices in efficiency as each segment creates its own staff functions, though the demands on the culture are not as great. There's also a danger that the segment CEOs could manage their assigned segments as freestanding silos, uninterested in cooperating with the others; such behavior would lead to trouble, since customers often migrate between segments, a process that should remain unhindered for the good of the company. In this vein it's interesting to note that Fidelity recently adopted what it calls a streamlined structure in which some functions, such as marketing, move to an internal service bureau model to reduce costs.

Thus we can identify two dimensions of continuity. The first is the degree of customer centricity, from bogus to complete. The second dimension is the degree of centralization of resources, from completely shared to completely decentralized. Since potential dangers exist at either end of this second dimension, the firm's economics and culture will determine the optimal position between the extremes. But it's obvious we believe in moving as far as possible toward the complete customer-centricity end of the first dimension. It gives a company by far its best shot at creating and executing the most competitively dominant value propositions and deriving maximum economic profit from its customers. The reason is that it's the only way it's absolutely clear who "owns" the customer.

How Structure Leads to Better Value Propositions

When accountable executives own the customers, all sorts of behavior starts changing almost immediately. Segment CEOs realize that their careers depend on the Customer Segment Value Creation Scorecard, so they focus intently on every cell in that spreadsheet. They start asking questions, of which the first is typically: Which customers in my segment are profitable and which are unprofitable? Then: Why—what are their characteristics? Why am I losing customers? Why is it costing so much to acquire them? Why aren't more of them buying our high-margin services?

These questions inevitably get managers thinking about the real keys to the kingdom: value propositions. You may recall that in the first chapter, Principle Three said better value propositions are the way successful companies outdo competitors and make their shares go up. Although we'll come back to discuss Value Proposition Management in much more detail in Chapters 7 and 8, we can begin to see the role of organizational structure in making this work. Creating, communicating, and executing effective value propositions are the activities at the very heart of the segment CEO's job.

Much of the power of organizing around customers derives from the fact that customer segment CEOs will be driven to create value propositions specifically for their segments. This is a big step forward for most companies. Since the typical organizational structure puts no one specifically and fully in charge of particular customers, the value propositions—the essential and all-important offers to those customers—tend to be fuzzy, ill-defined, even meaningless. Challenged to enunciate their value proposition, most companies struggle to say something that will apply to all their customers and end up with a bunch of air-filled blather about world-class quality, service, responsiveness, etc. But when a manager is explicitly in charge of a customer segment and realizes that increasing the economic profit from that segment is his job, then his focus on the customer value proposition suddenly becomes sharp and clear. He realizes that his value proposition must be tailored to the needs of his segment and can differ significantly from those being offered to the company's other customer segments. And he realizes it must be sharply defined and effectively executed because he's continually in competition with other segment CEOs for corporate resources to invest in his segment. In this way he is striving to create a premium P/E business unit within the broader corporation.

As a result of being organized around customers, with specific managers in charge of customer segments, the company changes from typically having one vague and forgettable customer value proposition to having many crisp, focused ones. Since value propositions are the soul of a business's success or failure, this is huge progress.

Notice what is happening. The segment CEOs immediately, naturally start trying to learn more about the traits, behaviors, needs, and desires of their customers—whatever they may be—and then casting an eye over the entire company, or even outside the company, as they try to develop value propositions that will keep profitable customers, acquire new ones, and make all customers more profitable. The segment managers actually want customer data; they thirst for it and will pay for it. This isn't too surprising until you reflect that at most companies today, customer data gets pushed at product and territory managers who aren't sure what to do with it, don't really want it, and certainly won't vote to spend the money to invest in it. Someone in the company realizes it's valuable and wants to see it used—a laudable sentiment—but because of the organizational structure, no one wants to use it. Instead of corporate task forces laboring over how best to use the data, the segment CEOs are powerfully incentivized to use it in precisely the ways that will create the most effective value propositions for the company. Data push gets transformed into data pull.

Having all of this customer-specific information for a segment centralized in a business unit ensures that customers are broadly owned. In the more traditional structure, all customer intelligence is collected on a hit-or-miss basis by a salesperson. That person might or might not do a good job. If she is very effective, then the risk is that if she were to leave, all the institutional knowledge and the relationships would leave as well. Again this argues strongly that a customer-centered organization will find it easier to produce much longer durations for earning positive spreads from customers and hence achieve turbocharged P/Es.

All of this behavior is exactly the reverse of the process at most companies, in which managers—no matter how much rah-rah customer-first indoctrination they've received—are ultimately responsible for a product-, function-, or territory-based P&L. To take the most common situation, a manager is trying to maximize the profitability of a product, not a customer segment, and is therefore certain to be missing opportunities. Think of it this way:

> In a product-centered company, a manager has an answer—a product—and is seeking customers with the right question. In a customer-centered company, a manager has customers with specific needs and is seeking winning value propositions for them.

In general, valuable resources, including customer data, will just lie there until someone can see exactly how to make money from them. That understanding becomes wonderfully clear when segment CEOs are paid on the basis of segment value creation.

Top Management's New Job

In a customer-centered company, top management takes on an important new dual responsibility: deciding where to place his or her organization on the spectrums of customer centricity and centralization of resources. With regard to the former, it's also necessary to choose the number and nature of customers' segment business units. How companies define their customer segments is a critical subject that we'll take up in the next chapter, but it's worth noting here that top-level executives will have to take a direct role in defining segments, which is a job for which they may feel unprepared. Customer segmentation at many companies is quite gross and unsophisticated. For example, a telecommunications company may divide customers into individuals and businesses. Further subdividing those two gigantic segments and giving managers responsibility for all segments is guaranteed to increase economic profit and the firm's value. At the other extreme, it is possible, though rare in practice, for a company to subdivide segments too finely, so that the cost of serving each segment becomes greater than the incremental benefit of focusing on the unique needs of a smaller group. So-called one-to-one marketing sounds great, and in the Internet age it seems tantalizingly close. But as a practical matter it still isn't feasible in most companies, at least in most companies that have large numbers of customers. The issues of developing and executing individual value propositions, which may involve customized inventories, production, billing, and other functions, are often just too overwhelming and usually—very important—too costly.

Finding the happy medium, the just-right number of segments, thus becomes one of top management's key jobs in a customer-centered company. Realize that this is always an iterative process. No company has ever defined its customer segments exactly right on the first try, and no company ever will. The best practice is to get started, start learning, and adjust the segments as experience dictates. The advantage will go to the company that begins this process first.

A caveat: Top management must be continually vigilant so that in creating customer segment business units, it doesn't simply replace product, territory, or functional silos with a new variation, since customer segments are always changing and customers often move from one segment to another. It's critical to avoid segment CEOs battling to hold on to profitable customers and to ship out unprofitable ones. Royal Bank of Canada's retail operation has segmented largely on a life-cycle basis, as we'll discuss in the next section, so it needs a smooth transition of customers from the young (and not very profitable) segments to the older (and far more profitable) segments. Vice chairman Jim Rager has done a highly effective job of creating a culture of collaboration.

A New Role for Product Managers

At this point we can hear you asking: But what about product managers? Put customer segment managers in charge if you like, but how could a company operate without product managers? What becomes of them?

The answer is that of course they have a role, a vitally important one, but different from their previous role. Above all they are internal suppliers to the customer segment managers—a big change, but it makes sense. Returning again to fundamental principles, a company exists not to sell products but to serve customers, and if the segment managers can't find a way to serve customers profitably with one of the company's products, then why is the company making that product at all? In our language from above, product managers become a centralized resource and certainly one of the most important in many companies. Here once again, top management must decide how centralized to make product management.

Note that it's entirely possible for a product-centric company to be making a product that all customer segment managers would find to be unprofitable, even though the company thought the product was profitable. The explanation, as you may have suspected from our discussion of the Customer Segment Value Creation Scorecard, is that in figuring product costs, a product-centric company rarely includes all the associated customer-specific costs or invested capital; for example, a type of insurance policy may get sold primarily to customers who respond well to expensive house calls by service reps who sell other products as well, or a media company may sell advertising to car dealerships that are especially slow in paying and require large investments in accounts receivable, or a retailer may sell a kind of golf club that appeals especially to elderly golfers, who consume a great deal of salespeople's time and attention. But in a customer-centered company those customer costs and capital get matched properly with revenues.

Product managers are still accountable for product P&Ls, properly calculated with all appropriate customer costs, as noted above. That's because they must be incentivized to supply their internal customers at reasonable cost, and they must be responsible for earning a satisfactory return on the company's investment in products. They remain the company's product experts, a necessary and vital role.

Problem: Most Companies Are Managed for the Managers

All these advantages, yet still most companies aren't organizing around customers. Why not? One reason, which is nothing to be proud of but is undeniable, is that many managers do what's convenient for them rather than what's convenient for customers. Jay Galbraith, a management professor at the International Institute for Management Development in Switzerland, points out that

> today, the preferred way is to "keep it simple"—create simple, autonomous business units which control their resources and which can be accountable for their performance. We also believe in keeping it simple, but with the twist that we want to "keep it simple for the customer." Organizations should be designed to do business in the way that the customer wants to do business. And how do customers want to do business? They want solutions that are seamlessly integrated across the products of multiple business units and countries.[4]

Back at the Bank of Outer Mongolia, you recall, the operating executives may have been clueless about their problem, but their boss wasn't. Remember what he said? That he realized there was a problem and he'd love to fix it, but the heads of the product fiefs were against any of the proposed changes, and they had a lot of organizational clout. Result: He didn't even try to change, and a bad situation stayed that way.

Here we find the number one reason more companies are not organizing around customers. They don't even try. Typically they have the customer data they need, or they could get it, and they have the necessary computers and software or could get them; they understand why the change would be a good idea. But they just don't try it. This is a crucial point. It's not that companies by the thousand are trying and failing to do this. On the contrary, the failure rate for this kind of transformation is not terribly high. Rather, most companies haven't even tried to organize themselves around customers, and of those that consider it, many back off without starting down the road.

The reason they don't try it is that it would mean changing who's accountable for what. We cannot overstate the importance of this fact of organizational life. No other type of change in an enterprise holds so much potential to spark opposition, from foot-dragging to open rebellion. Not only is such a change large and therefore daunting, it also goes to the heart of organizational power and politics. That's why Brad Anderson, CEO of Best Buy—a retailing leader who has started down the road of making his organization truly customer-centered—says this change is analogous to the disruptive technologies identified by Harvard Business School professor Clayton Christiansen in his book, *The Innovator's Dilemma.* Like those technologies, becoming customer-centered is so far outside the mental models of many executives that they can't see any potential value in it. They are far more comfortable with adjusting the status quo incrementally, and in doing so they may be marching toward their own demise, like Kmart.

The concept of the innovator's dilemma furnishes an important warning for the customer-centered company. Such a company may focus on those customers in deciles 1 and 2, as measured by economic profit or return on invested capital. The temptation to shunt off decile 10 customers will be strong. But a start-up competitor may be able to create a winning value proposition for that group. Who cares? says the dominant incumbent. But the new competitor may then be able to adapt its new value proposition and business model to attack decile 9, then decile 8, and so on. Before long, the dominant incumbent faces a grave threat, which it barely saw coming, to the decile 1 and 2 customers that are the foundation of its business. It happens all the time. Think of Dell Computer, which now very profitably rules the huge business of selling computers to companies, but fifteen years ago was focused on the consumer market, which the dominant incumbents (IBM, Hewlett-Packard, Compaq) saw as small potatoes.

In general, opposition from the heads of existing fiefdoms is the biggest obstacle to true customer centricity because it's motivated by a direct threat to the power of powerful executives; their reaction can be almost primal, and that's a fearsome thing. It's enough to scare a CEO. Some corporate chiefs have told us they'd be willing to take on fiefdom heads one at a time. But a change like this would require taking on all of them at once—and that's just too big a fight. Of course the fact that resistance may be intense should not stop a chief executive who has concluded that the change is the right move, but it frequently does. Remember the fact we reported earlier, that some 60 percent of companies fail the most fundamental test of management because they don't earn their cost of capital or just barely do so? This inability to do what needs doing because of internal opposition is one of the major reasons. That's why facing the reality of becoming customer-centered can be such a crucible for top leadership.

Complicating matters are other obstacles that sometimes arise when a company contemplates the reality of becoming truly customer-centered. We've encountered all of these objections:

> ⅄ Organizing around customers may actually conflict with
> a company's culture, with its view of "who we are." Despite
> decades of executive obeisance to the importance of customer
> service, the fact is many people still don't think of service as
> the highest calling in business. A number of great companies
> were founded on other ideals that on their own may be highly
> laudable. Some, like Motorola, Texas Instruments, and
> Hewlett-Packard, are all about great engineering—that's the
> highest value in the company. Others, like Merck and
> Amgen, are all about great science. Still others, like Microsoft
> and Nike, were built as competitive killing machines, focused

on annihilating competitors. Organizing around customers, with all the new priorities that follow naturally from it, is such a different way to see the world that it may provoke a corporate identity crisis.

∀   Managers may object that true customer centricity is all fine in theory but unworkable in practice. The reason, they insist, is that measuring the performance of customer-based managers is impossible. As we've seen and will see further, that just isn't true.

∀   Managers sometimes say the company can't afford to make the needed computer and software fixes. This objection is clever because it hits most top executives in a weak spot: They don't know much about computing or its costs, and experience has made them all too fearful of information technology projects that destroy the budget, so underlings see an opportunity to snow the boss. Yet as we've seen, it's possible for a company to get hugely valuable data about customer profitably through sampling, without any extra IT spending at all. Moving beyond sampling to really thorough analysis of customer segmentation and customer profitability probably will require additional IT spending, but the IT guys know it can be done. Top executives are better off getting their advice about this from their own IT department, not from operating managers with turf to defend.

∀   Managers sometimes object that the change would be too disruptive to the organization and its customers. As a result, they argue, customers wouldn't benefit, they'd actually suffer if the company tried this. We have to admire this objection for its audacity. When the boss proposes reorganizing the whole company so that everything revolves around identifying and creatively satisfying the needs of every customer in a profitable way, it takes some nerve to argue that this would make customers worse off.

⋎   Managers may complain that the company is too busy with other urgent priorities, such as integrating an acquisition. In other words, organizing around customers is important, but other things—namely, whatever problems we're dealing with right now—are more important.

⋎   Managers may demand to know how they can be sure the change will work. Never mind that in the rest of their business and personal lives they move with alacrity on mere shards of information, buying stocks on tips from neighbors and engaging consultants after hearing a good speech. When it comes to an idea that could change their role in the corporation, they won't be convinced if you can't give them a triple-A–rated promise.

⋎   Most insidiously, managers may appear to accept the change but resist passively, for example, by planning a transition that would take a decade. Don't laugh—we've seen it happen.

Understand that the change can be made; a number of companies have made it, and more are doing so now. But you can see why one of the comments we've heard most frequently at companies that have made themselves truly customer-centered is, "This would be a lot easier if the company had been organized like this from the beginning."

In Chapter 9 we'll go into the how-to of making an organization customer-centered. But those specific issues won't make sense until we understand more precisely what the customer-centered organization has to accomplish. So let's turn to that next.

△ 6 ▽

The Right Way to Segment Customers

Reconceiving Your Company
as a Customer Portfolio

Perhaps at this point you're ready to accept Principle One, that your company, like all companies, is a portfolio of customers, and that organizing around these customers is the right way to go. In accepting that principle, defining customer segments is where the rubber meets the road. Now it's time to get into the nuts and bolts of making it happen, and that has to begin with defining the customer segments. Don't doubt the value of this exercise. Done properly, it confers enormous competitive advantages. It becomes the foundation of the corporate architecture. It is decidedly worth the effort it takes. Expert segmentation has been a significant though little-known factor in the success of Dell Computer, for example. As former CFO Tom Meredith says, "Being segmented against a competitor who isn't—that's nirvana."

Customer segmentation is a familiar concept, but few companies have segmented customers on the basis of any understanding of customer profitability, and even fewer have really implemented segmentation. That means most companies haven't segmented customers in the way that would maximize shareowner value creation. It also means that much of the conventional wisdom about how to segment customers—such as categorizing them by age or income—is often badly misleading. In other words, it's time to rethink customer segmentation in a way that will build more value.

Even if you find the concept of segmenting intuitive, the method of doing it is anything but. For example, suppose your local supermarket decides to put customers at the center and classify all its customers into segments. What's the best approach? If the manager used conventional criteria, he might decide to segment customers by age—so that you would be in, say, the forty to fifty segment. Or maybe segmenting by family composition would make more sense, putting you in the families-with-teenagers segment. Or maybe it's smarter to segment by annual household income, with you in the $80,000–$100,000 group. Or it might be better to segment by average purchase, so you'd be in the $60–$75 segment.

It isn't hard to cook up a cogent argument for segmenting along any of these dimensions or several others you could probably imagine. The trouble is segmentation isn't worth much unless the results are actionable. But what do we mean by actionable? Actually, three highly interrelated dimensions make a segmentation actionable. First, the segmentation has to be actionable from the customer's perspective—i.e., it has to deal with what matters most to customers, their **needs**. Those needs include both cost and noncost needs. Second, if we put customers into different segment buckets and then take actions to provide them with experiences that better meet their needs, we have to be able to track and understand their individual **behavior**. So the segmentation we choose must enable us to "mark" individual customers and observe whether our efforts result in more visits to our store, increased conversion rate of leads to sales, or larger, more profitable bundles of goods being purchased. Finally, we have to be able to measure the profitability of the customer segments and ensure that we are focusing our efforts on customers which offer the greatest **profit**. Too often in companies, we encounter customer segments developed by marketing departments using general demographic or psychographic characteristics. Unfortunately, since they are laboring in noncustomer-centered organizations, they don't have the mandate to really drive the business by segments. The end result is that they have no facts on the profitability of the segments and often have to rely on anecdotal evidence for how their segments are responding to various marketing stimuli. All of this reinforces the reluctance of the rest of the organization to support initial steps toward becoming customer-centered.

Of these three different dimensions, our two primary bases for segmentation are needs and profitability. We focus on needs—not customer income, age, attitudes, zip code, occupation, marital status, or any of the other criteria by which businesses typically analyze customers, but needs. In practice some of those conventional criteria may help a company gain insights into customer needs and behavior, as we shall see, but exactly how will differ from company to company. The key principle is sufficiently clear that we can use it to define a customer segment:

> A customer segment is a group of customers with sufficiently homogeneous needs that the segment members can be won with a common value proposition and common marketing.

Imagine a company that has 1 million customers, and suppose the company identifies ten candidate customer segments. Each segment meets the above definition to varying degrees. At the same time each segment will be characterized by current profitability and future profit potential or value, which will also vary among the candidate segments. How should management decide on a set of target segments? We have found the Segmentation Matrix a very useful tool.

Imagine placing all the candidate customer segments on the grid.

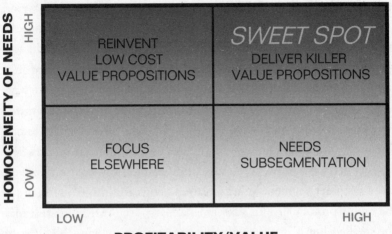

SEGMENTATION MATRIX

HOMOGENEITY OF NEEDS

HIGH	REINVENT LOW COST VALUE PROPOSITIONS	*SWEET SPOT* DELIVER KILLER VALUE PROPOSITIONS
LOW	FOCUS ELSEWHERE	NEEDS SUBSEGMENTATION

LOW   HIGH

PROFITABILITY/VALUE

Nirvana is in the northeast quadrant—a very high degree of homogeneity of needs and a very high level of profitability. The case for winning, retaining, and growing these segments is clear. Because they have highly similar needs, one well-crafted, communicated, and executed value proposition should add tons of economic profit and drive the company's share price. This would seem to be a highly attractive segment to target right away. Segments in the southwest quadrant are characterized by a mixed bag of customers in terms of needs and with little profit opportunity. This is probably not a place to begin focusing resources. Indeed after all of the target segments have been selected, we have found it useful to place all nonsegmented customers into one bucket, called "other." In most instances, one would expect "other" to be in the southwest.

Suppose the company with 1 million customers has created a segment comprised of about 200,000 small business customers, and the profitability of those customers is quite high. But because the customers seem to have divergent needs, the segment scores low in homogeneity and thus sits in the southeast quadrant. The low degree of homogeneity reduces the likelihood of finding a value proposition that will satisfy most of the segment. Yet its high profitability suggests that subsegmenting the segment into several camps might yield several new segments that have a higher degree of homogeneity and thus are more susceptible to a common value proposition. When we have done this in practice, it is very common for some of the subsegments to move to other quadrants. For instance, one subsegment of small business customers may be very interested in using our services and intellectual capital. As we discussed in Chapter 4 in connection with the Customer Segment Value Creation Scorecard, those offerings can be highly profitable. This subsegment charges to the northeast. It may be smaller, but it is very profitable and more easily winnable. Part of the small business subsegment may move to the southwest, suggesting not a lot of attention for the present. Another portion of small business may move to the northwest quadrant. Suppose the subsegmentation has succeeded in identifying a group of perhaps 75,000 customers with very common needs, but at this point we can't make money with them meeting those needs. This is the place to figure out how to meet their needs with perhaps a different service or delivery channel. Ignoring this quadrant might result in management becoming a victim of the Innovator's Dilemma discussed in the previous chapter.

But we are getting ahead of ourselves. First the company has to work on its segmentation—understanding needs and profitability. Next, it looks at behavior in order to understand the profitability of the segment; think back to our previous discussions of the Bank of Outer Mongolia and our retailer, both of which had profitable as well as unprofitable customers. It is important to stress that this is an iterative process—creating candidate segments, creating new or refining existing value propositions, and then using the Customer Segment

Value Creation Scorecard to ensure that the customer segment team is progressing in its goal to create a sustained premium P/E business.

Before we get into how to determine those all-important needs and group them most usefully, note that our customer segment definition leaves us a lot of leeway. It's useful to consider the extremes. For example, a computer company could divide its customers into just two segments, individuals and businesses, each with millions of members. Does each group have sufficiently homogeneous needs to be susceptible to common offers and marketing? Individuals in general will be interested in ease of setup and use, while businesses in general will be interested in networking, system support, and scalability. So dividing those millions of customers into just two huge segments would appear to satisfy our definition. And on the whole, creating offers for each of those two segments based on those interests would probably be more effective than making the same offers to everyone. But these needs will no doubt turn out to be very high level and not especially homogeneous. Ease of use could vary widely, depending for instance on whether the user is interested in applications for entertainment or for personal finance.

At the other extreme, the same company could define each and every customer as a segment—millions of customers, millions of segments. In that case, are each segment's needs homogeneous? Absolutely, it would seem. They literally couldn't be any more homogeneous, could they? Even here we have not completed the possible levels of subsegmentation. Are you the same customer by time of day, on weekdays versus on weekends, at home versus on the road? The 7-Eleven Japan chain of convenience stores has made a real science of understanding these nuances, resulting in different offers at different times of day. So the possibilities for subsegmentation are truly endless.

Some companies have so few customers that making each customer a segment is only sensible. If you sell to the world's major airframe manufacturers or automakers or jet engine builders or investment banks or pharmaceutical companies, segments of one may make perfect sense. Even in these cases, remember that there may still be some cats and dogs, and the use of "other" as a holding pen can be helpful.

In practice, most companies will have to find a degree of segmentation between these two extremes. The trade-off is obvious: Finer segmentation, because it focuses more precisely on customer needs, leads to better-crafted and more differentiated value propositions, and thus typically to greater acceptance, higher margins, increased loyalty, and higher economic profit. On the other hand, it typically involves higher costs. At some point adding more segments adds incremental costs that wipe out gains in economic profit. These added costs can come in the form of complexity in the supply chain or higher purchasing costs due to lost standardization. Graphically this relationship is a curve:

OPTIMAL NUMBER OF SEGMENTS

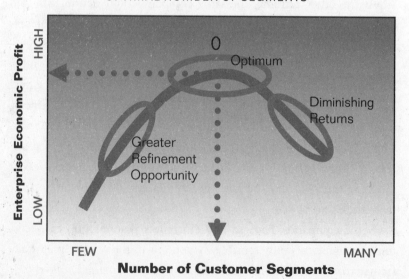

One of top management's most important jobs—but a job most top management doesn't do today—is to put the company at point O on the graph, the degree of optimal customer segmentation. The great majority of companies are far to the left of point O and will find that finer segmentation will lead to higher profitability. For example, Dell's longtime policy was to subdivide a customer segment whenever its annual revenues reached $500 million. Fidelity Investments used to classify customers into just three age segments (less than 36 years old, 36–60 years old, and more than 60 years old) and by two asset segments (less than $100,000 and more than $100,000). Now it uses six main segments, described below, the largest of which is divided into ten subsegments. Margins have improved dramatically as a result because the company can tailor products, services, delivery channels, and prices in a more differentiated way to make all its customers more profitable.

How does this discussion of the optimal number of segments connect to the previous discussion about focusing on the highest profit segments in our Segmentation Matrix? Clearly if top management focuses on segments with the highest profit and highest potential, the above curve may shift to the right and upward. That is, if the company is particularly effective at identifying the most valuable segments, then the optimal point, O, will occur where the company has designated more customer segments and is earning more economic profit as a result. It's still subject to diminishing returns from segmenting too finely, but the better it is at identifying the sweet spot on the Segmentation Matrix, the greater its economic profit opportunity will be.

You've Got to Start Someplace

In defining customer segments there are many places to begin. Wherever you begin, keep in mind that you'll never get it perfect. There are too many ways to do it, too many factors to consider, and the world is too dynamic. The process demands imagination and creativity; it's art as well as science. The scope of the project overwhelms some companies. They fall into analysis paralysis, so determined to get it exactly right that they never get anywhere at all. This is fatal. The key is to get the segmenation generally right and move forward, quickly. As IBM's greatest leader, Thomas Watson, Jr., used to say, "It's not so important which decision is made as *that* a decision is made. If it's wrong, it will come back to bite us soon enough, and we can fix it." The same goes for defining customer segments.

Competitively superior customer segmentation is a five-step process:

1. Grouping all customers into deciles by profitability
2. Studying customer behavior within these profitability deciles to begin to understand why some customers are more profitable than others
3. Using this understanding, defining needs-based segments
4. Dividing each of these segments into profitability deciles
5. Based on experience over time, redefining or subdividing segments

In Chapter 3 we discussed the power of deaveraging. As we saw, deciles 1 and 2 (the most profitable) and decile 10 (the least) are hugely important to the overall performance of the company. So in defining customer segments, it's vital to understand the behavior of customers in these extreme groups. That's where to begin your search for segment candidates. We emphasize that these deciles will *not* be your customer segments. But identifying these deciles, and then examining the behavior of customers within them, is a great way to start. It's a particularly useful way to develop insights for identifying the segments that will be in the desirable northeast quadrant of the Segmentation Matrix. Step two then weaves in other information, such as customer behavior, to understand profitability differences and develop segment candidates. Incorporating demographic and attitudinal research leads to further refinement of the segments, including hypotheses about customer needs (met and unmet).

Employees who are deeply familiar with the business and its customers can get together and talk it through. You can mine existing customer data to see what customers have told you about their needs—but with the huge caveat that customers often don't tell you the truth about this. You can ask customers about their needs through surveys and focus groups, but again remember that customers may not always realize their own needs. Most people didn't know they needed a cell phone until they saw one, but now millions of people insist they couldn't live without one. To complement asking customers for information, you can videotape their behavior. We've seen all these approaches used successfully. As you further refine the segment you want to begin profiling customers. Who are they? How would you know if you bumped into them?

Regardless of which approaches you use, it's important to remember that customer needs may not be apparent through their behavior and may not correspond with the products and services you currently offer. For example, we know a telephone company customer who recently bought a DSL line with a self-install kit. That observation on behavior, plus knowing that the customer is highly profitable, doesn't detect a vital fact: that he's terribly unhappy with his experience. He doesn't like dealing with wiring and software, and he faces many demands on his time. His need isn't a product. His need is to have fast on-line access with a minimum use of his time. The behavioral observations that he's profitable and bought the product doesn't address his key unmet need, which could be very profitably met by the phone company.

When you begin sketching the outlines of what your customers need relative to the business you're in, you will discover that these needs fall into a number of groups. For the hypothetical supermarket mentioned above, some customers need the lowest prices. Others need to get in and out fast. Others need to shop at odd hours, while still others need unusual specialty foods. Some customers will have more than one of these needs. For the supermarket's managers, it's important to understand the relative strength of these needs and, ultimately, which can be met profitably and which can't. Meeting a need often adds costs.

One reason successful segmenting is so challenging is that it's rarely possible to know with certainty a customer's needs based on the available information about that customer. Companies therefore look for customer traits that are the best available *proxies* for customer needs. For example, the supermarket owner cannot know for sure which customers will most want to get through the store quickly. But if he knows that a customer is part of a family with kids and spends over $150 a week at the supermarket—information about the customer that is readily available through a combination of the supermarket's own data, gathered through credit card or loyalty card analysis, plus third party data—then it's good bet this customer is time-pressed and is spending a lot of hours in the store, and thus feels a strong need to save time. Yet it could also be that some families regard a trip to the supermarket as a kind of family outing, with no particular time pressure. Understanding customer behavior is obviously critical to understanding their needs and choosing the most profitable response.

Different companies use different proxies for customer needs, and within a company these proxies need not always be along the same dimension. For example, the retail division of Fidelity Investments, the world's largest mutual fund company, segments customers primarily—but not entirely—by the amount of money they have invested with the firm. Here is how Fidelity defines its customers segments:

Private Access	over $2 million invested with the firm
Premium	$500,000 to $2 million invested with the firm
Preferred	$100,000 to $500,000 invested with the firm
Core	less than $100,000 invested with the firm
Basic	unprofitable because of calling patterns
Active Traders	trade more than 36 times per year

Note that the first four segments are defined by assets. The Basic segment, however, is defined by unprofitability for a particular reason—these customers spend so much time on the phone with the call centers or with their local Fidelity office that they are unprofitable for Fidelity. When it comes to needs, these customers have a powerful need to talk. The Active Trader segment is defined by behavior. That's not inconsistency, it's just one way of getting at customer needs in a way that's highly actionable. One can well imagine further subsegmenting, perhaps on the basis of complexity of a customer's trading—for example, exotic options plays versus plain vanilla S&P 500 stock trading.

But doesn't this lead to segment overlap? It could, but Fidelity doesn't allow it. An important principle of segmentation we've observed at every company that does it successfully is that *segments are mutually exclusive:* Every customer is assigned to one and only one segment. Most of those Active Traders would qualify for one of the asset-defined segments, but Fidelity puts them solely into the Active Trader segment. It believes that's the best way to meet their most important needs. And—at least as important—there's no question about which segment manager is responsible for them.

In a completely different business, another very customer-centered company, Dell Computer, also segments customers along differing dimensions in order to meet their most important needs. Here are Dell's segments in its business-to-business operations; each of these six segments is divided further into subsegments:

1. Small Business
2. Medium and Large Business
3. State and Local Government
4. Federal Government
5. Education
6. Health Care

Again we see potential overlap; education could be part of state and local government, and a health care establishment, depending on its type, could conceivably be in any of the government or business segments. But Dell also assigns each customer to one and only one segment. It's interesting to note that Dell didn't categorize its business and government customers into segments before 1993; until then it was focused on selling PCs to individuals and had categorized these customers into seven segments. Examples: Techno-Wizards, who were insensitive to price and just wanted the latest and greatest technology; and Techno-Phobes, who needed lots and lots of technical support. Then the company noticed that its business customers could be usefully segmented as well. Former CFO Tom Meredith observes, "Every time we segmented more finely, the new segment grew faster."

In defining segments, Dell believes the best proxy for a customer's needs is the kind of business or government unit a customer is in, while Fidelity believes the best proxy for its customers' needs is the dollar size of their relationship with the firm, or in some cases their financial behavior. Are they right? It's impossible to say with certainty. What we can say for sure is that no rule for determining the best proxy applies to all industries, and that finding an appropriate proxy is a critically important first step in segmentation. We can also say that both firms are achieving clear, substantial gains from their segmentation efforts, suggesting that their different bases for segmenting are certainly valuable stages of development, and that both firms are constantly reexamining their segmentation decisions to see if they can be improved. We strongly suspect, based on the evidence of many companies, that *any* serious basis for segmentation according to needs, once implemented, can yield clear benefits in profitability and value creation because it starts getting resources allocated better and creates clear accountability for results. Once needs-based segments have been targeted, it is extraordinarily useful to re-decile each segment. Within a given segment, are the profitability deciles as extreme as in the overall company? Why or why not? Do these insights suggest subsegments that could be located more favorably on the Segmentation Matrix? Again, what are the key differences in behaviors, attitudes, and perhaps needs of customers in deciles 1, 2, and 10? Finally, the segment definitions can be refined and improved. The key, then, is to get the process started and put into action.

How a Champion at Segmentation Did It

Royal Bank's segmenting experience illustrates a number of important points. The company's personal and commerical banking division began its effort by surveying customers about what they wanted, and what they felt they were getting, from banks. In other words, Royal Bank decided to learn about customer needs in the most direct way: by asking customers. The answers were intriguing. Customers wanted all the usual services and competencies one expects from a bank—reliability, convenience, the conventional banking products. But customers also felt that virtually every bank was providing these just fine. These were the usual, familiar criteria by which banks judged themselves, so most banks were attempting to compete on these issues. Trouble was, customers barely cared.

But Royal Bank also found that customers deeply wanted other things, which together might be called a relationship. Specifically, they wanted a bank to show that it appreciated and valued the customer's business; they wanted to be treated as individuals not account numbers; they wanted the bank to demonstrate that it knew them; and they wanted the bank to anticipate their needs. Further, they wanted the bank to do all this in every form of interaction—at the branch, on the phone, on-line, by mail. Royal Bank found that no bank in Canada was even close to delivering these customer needs, so it decided to base its strategy on meeting them.

Among personal clients (as distinct from businesses), Royal Bank concluded that the best basis for segmenting in order to meet customers' needs for a relationship was life stage. That's a conventional basis for segmentation, but Royal Bank adopted it with a twist. Most people's banking needs change in a fairly predictable way over the course of their lives, so the basic approach made sense; if you want to anticipate a customer's banking needs, you've got a big head start if you know she's a twenty-two-year-old recent college graduate or a sixty-two-year-old recent retiree. But simply knowing a customer's age and employment status isn't enough. Royal Bank found that in some life stages, it's important to distinguish subgroups characterized by different behaviors, which the bank labeled High and Low. The result was eight primary segments:

1. Youth	less than 18 years old
2. Nexus	18 to 35 years old; single, or married without children
3. Builders and Borrowers—High	more loans than investments; family-centric; building for the future; average age 40
4. Builders and Borrowers—Low	many more loans than investments; living for today; fewer children
5. Wealth Accumulators—High	more investments than loans; worried about retirement; looking to clear debts
6. Wealth Accumulators—Low	similar to above, but fewer assets
7. Wealth Preservers—High	living off investments; looking to maintain living standards and maintain emergency funds
8. Wealth Preservers—Low	similar to above, but fewer assets

No matter what needs-based segments a company defines, it's important to be sure they're congruent with customer behavior, not just with what customers say. The reason is that customers frequently do not walk their talk. At Royal Bank, for example, a high proportion of customers—nearly half—said they would prefer to acquire loans and investments on-line. They could do so if they liked, but very few actually did it.

Like all companies that create significant value through customer segmentation, Royal Bank deciles its primary segments by profitability just as in our earlier discussion. This is important in two ways.

First, as we have stressed, profitability is a highly useful basis for analyzing a customer segment, but *not* for primary segmenting. Royal Bank discovered a principle that appears to be universal: Segments based on profitability do not share homogeneous needs. That's just common sense. It's easy to imagine how a family breadwinner with a big mortgage and a retiree with large cash balances would both be highly profitable for a bank, quite possibly landing in the same profitability decile. But putting them into the same customer segment probably wouldn't help a bank create many new service opportunities that would delight both customers.

Nonetheless, many companies continue to segment customers by profitability, or, even more illogically, by revenue. For example, Gail McGovern, who was so successful leading the customer-centricity revolution at Fidelity, was previously an executive at AT&T. She reports that AT&T would segment customers by how much they spent—say those who spent over $75 a month and those who spent less—but found that road warriors had much more in common with one another, regardless of how much they spent, than they had in common with others in their spending category. So: Segment by needs and use profitability as a key tool to understand and refine the needs-based segments.

Second, it's extremely important to know the profitability of all the customers within a needs-based segment. The reason is that these customer segment deciles can differ enormously and knowledge of this may lead to richer subsegmentation. For example, Fidelity's core segment includes customers who maintain nearly $500,000 of mutual fund balances and never touch them; they're highly profitable. It also includes a customer who telephoned the firm 9,300 times in one year; he's highly unprofitable. The firm can't hope to create maximum value from segmentation until it understands who these customers are, recognizes their diverse needs, and determines how to treat them differently.

A Closer Look at Step 4: Similar Needs, Widely Varying Profitability

When we talk about Step Four in the segmenting process, dividing needs-based segments into deciles based on profitability, we mean (just as in Step 1) economic profitability—that is, the amount by which the dollar return on invested capital exceeds the dollar cost of capital. This will be a switch for some companies, which are more comfortable in their segmentation analyses looking at operating margins or related measures. For companies still in the dark ages of segmenting by revenue instead of needs, this is even more important. A major retailer still segments customers by the amount they charge on their store credit card. But the payment behavior of these customers is actually far more important, because the store makes far greater profits on customers who pay off their balances slowly. So a low-spending customer who pays over many months may be much more profitable than a big spender who pays off the balance in full each month. Remember, your whole object is to create shareowner value, and you simply cannot know if you are succeeding unless you are measuring economic profitability. And yes, you do have all the data you need in order to calculate these numbers or at least approximate them on a sample basis; it's just a matter of getting started.

As often as we repeat that customer profitability distributions are usually extreme, people are still amazed by what they find within their own companies. For example, when Fidelity subdivided its main customer segments into profitability deciles, it found that *every* segment included unprofitable customers. That even included the company's most affluent segment, Private Access, all members of which maintained at least $2 million of assets with Fidelity. Managers were shocked to find that 10 percent of these customers were unprofitable. Of course the company quickly set about learning why, and then sought to make the unprofitable customers profitable.

Issues of customer profitability can be far more subtle than just who's profitable and who isn't, as we'll see in later chapters. For example, an operator of gas stations may identify a customer segment based on the need to get in and out quickly. Within that segment, he may find there are two subgroups of differing profitability: limo drivers, who buy huge volumes of gasoline and are highly profitable, and young moms, who are much less profitable. If the station operator's response is to create a special quick-turnaround lane for this segment, and if it fills up with young moms, making the limo drivers unhappy, that's a problem. A more successful tactic might be a device like Exxon Mobil's Speedpass, which lets customers pay for their fill-up instantly by waving a small plastic token over the pump face, an innovation many other retailers could adopt. The point is that realizing the opportunities that arise from differing customer profitability isn't always easy, but you won't even know about these opportunities until you calculate customer profitability.

Once a company has classified customers into needs-based segments and has arrayed customers by profitability within segments, it can usefully subdivide these segments on many other dimensions as well. For example, Fidelity subdivides its largest segment, Core, with 4.2 million customers, into ten subsegments based on future opportunity. One subsegment is called Outside Brokerage—aha, here's an opportunity to attract a customer's brokerage business not currently with Fidelity. Another subsegment is called High Outside Assets— again, an obvious opportunity. And even with all that subsegmenting, there's no evidence Fidelity has gone too far—that it has moved past point 0, the optimal number of segments on our earlier chart.

A useful related dimension is potential profitability. Royal Bank rates all customers on this dimension, using predictive models that consider a wide range of customer data and that forecast the period each customer can be expected to stay with the bank, the products the customer will likely use over that period, and the profitability of those products. The bank has found that not all profitable customers have much potential, and some less profitable customers have a lot of potential. That information is highly valuable to segment managers deciding how much to spend in order to acquire and retain customers.

Similarly, a company could subdivide segments by:

ⵗ   customer vulnerability, meaning the odds he or she will defect to a competitor
ⵗ   channel preference
ⵗ   risk of nonpayment

or by many other criteria that would be useful to segment managers, depending on the nature of the business. All these criteria are already being used by companies. What they have in common is that they help the segment managers perceive new opportunities to create value for and from customers—current and potential—and help those managers allocate resources and take action to realize those opportunities.

Who's in Charge of Segmenting?

The actual exercise of defining segments can be carried out in any number of ways just as long as a company observes one rule, a rule many companies are tempted to flout: The people who will be accountable for customer segment performance must be in charge. Not consultants, not the marketing department, not even the CEO, but rather the managers who will be accountable for the results of segmenting must own the segment definitions. Accountability has to begin at the beginning. This way there's no buck-passing, no grousing that the idiots upstairs didn't know what they were doing.

For this reason we recommend that any company serious about putting customers at the center begin the segmenting process by identifying a cross-functional group of excellent managers and telling them that some of them are going to be the new customer segment CEOs. Their job, jointly, is to define the customer segments. They may well want to bring in consultants, marketing people, and computer specialists. For example, when Fidelity began the process, the managers sat down with the company's IT experts and listed some of the key things they'd like to know about their customers as a possible basis for segmentation. The IT staff then crunched the data and began to identify clusters, iterating back and forth with the managers.

Having selected *candidate* segments, each team is then required to prepare a Customer Segment Value Creation Scorecard based on the current set of customers in their segment. They are also charged with making a first pass at analyzing the value proposition being delivered to the segment and recommending changes based on their analysis.

Once the group has completed this work, top management names the segment managers. Each should be given a fairly brief time, say sixty days, to prepare the Customer Segment Value Creation Scorecard for his or her segment and initial value propositions for increasing the segment's economic profitability.

Inevitably, some segments will be more profitable than others. To prevent jockeying and politicking among the managers as they work on defining segments, top management must let them know that their success in eventually managing segments will be judged not by their segment's raw dollar profitability, but rather by increases in its profitability—specifically, increases as they translate into shareowner value. Thus, a negative-profit segment—which in the extreme case could create considerable value for the company simply by being shut down—may present as great an opportunity as a high-profit one.

*   *   *

It all depends on how successfully segment managers create competitively superior value for the customer segments they're dealt and as a consequence generate exceptional profit for shareowners. That crucial topic—how companies do it, step by step—is what we turn to next.

$\triangle$ 7 $\triangledown$

Knowing and Winning Customers

The Beginning of Value
Proposition Management

Say your company has settled on a portfolio of customer segments that it intends to keep and manage. That is, you've created customer segments teams, each one focused on creating a premium P/E business. They've worked through their respective Customer Segment Value Creation Scorecards and figured their current economic profit and what improvement is required to drive each customer business unit to a premium P/E.

Now the question is *how?*

Managing these segments optimally to realize their goals is all about a concept we've discussed but haven't yet addressed head-on: managing the company's value propositions. Now we're ready for that crucial step.

Because we believe this process is so important, we have given it a name: Value Proposition Management. VPM can best be understood in three broad stages: creation, communication, and execution of a value proposition. To succeed, you've got to be good at all three.

But what exactly is a value proposition? We think of it as the *complete experience* a company delivers to its customer.[1]

Imagine a lawyer, investment banker, or senior executive who frequently needs to fly from New York after a full workday for business meetings the next morning in London, and then return to New York for an evening board meeting. The needs of any customer in this segment are quite specific: saving time and getting rest. British Airways and American Airlines both offer value propositions—complete experiences—for these customers. The experience starts when the customer realizes the need to go to London and return for the next evening's meeting. The experience then comprises each interaction with the airline, beginning with making the reservation, then arriving at the airport, checking in, going through security, boarding the plane, eating, sleeping, deplaning, and going through customs in London, with most of the process repeated on the return flight. The final elements of the experience include the posting of the trip to the customer's frequent flier statement and the charge for the trip on the company's credit card. The complete experience is the value proposition. Each airline delivers one. The dominant or *winning* value proposition for the targeted customer segment is the one that best meets the full set of customer needs, including price.

It's important to realize that if you're in business, you have a value proposition—even if you've never thought about it before. Every business has one; most just aren't very good. Think back to the Dismal Dozen companies, those with consistently subpar P/Es, introduced in Chapter 1. No doubt you've bought some of their products or services. If you're like most people we talk to, you've not been thrilled, which is precisely why these companies are in the Dismal Dozen. If these companies consistently delivered much better experiences to their customers, they would certainly make significant progress toward realizing the $1 trillion opportunity we discussed in Chapters 1 and 4.

By contrast, consider the Dynamite Dozen. Some of them, such as Starbucks, Bed Bath & Beyond, and Wal-Mart, have created remarkably differentiated, winning value propositions. The fact that everyone knows exactly what the experience will be is a testimony to their success in communicating the value proposition. But VPM is more than just creation and communication. As a whole, the Dynamite Dozen companies are paragons of executional excellence. If your financial performance looks more like the Dismal Dozen than the Dynamite Dozen, then it's almost certain you've got serious work to do on at least one of the three stages of Value Proposition Management.

Success means achieving a mutually beneficial value exchange. You provide your customer with a complete experience, or value proposition, and your customer rewards you with an appropriate level of economic profit. The *Value Exchange Model* communicates this notion (see figure on page 142). Your company is in equilibrium with your customers when what you are giving customers matches up with the economic profit you are receiving back. Both the Dynamite Dozen and Dismal Dozen are in equilibrium: In each case the companies are getting what they deserve.

Through much of the discussions in Chapters 1 through 4, we challenged you to understand which of your customers are providing *you* with a beneficial value exchange in the form of strong economic profitability and which are not—understanding deeply the profitability performance of deciles 1 and 2 versus that of decile 10. Customers in deciles 1 and 2 are probably happy with their complete experience, resulting in a mutually beneficial value exchange. But it's unlikely the same is true for the decile 10 customers, whose poor profit performance suggests they're probably not receiving a satisfactory value proposition.

Customers with different needs will require different experiences, different value propositions, if the exchange is to be mutually beneficial. As the airline example illustrates, excellent value propositions don't exist at the corporate level or even at the product or service level.

Customer Centricity
Customer Value Exchange Model
Value Propositions

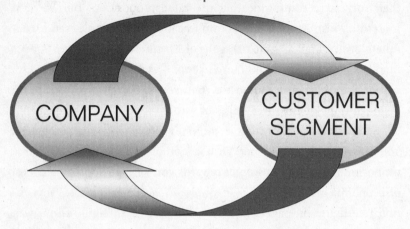

Economic Profit

They must exist at the customer segment level, with each segment characterized by specific, homogeneous needs. The London-bound businesspeople served by competing airlines provide a vivid example. On the matrix we introduced in Chapter 6, showing homogeneity of needs on one axis and profitability/value on the other, this segment sits in that desirable northeast corner, ranking high on both dimensions. In this context, the job of the customer segment CEO and her team is to understand deeply the needs of their segment, the relative importance of each need as perceived by the customer, and how well the most important needs are being met today by each competitor. Then the assignment is to create an experience that is competitively superior in meeting the customer segment's specific mix of cost and noncost needs. In general, customer business units that do this well will create a mutually beneficial value exchange—each based on a distinct value proposition.

No value proposition will succeed in delivering exceptional economic profit to a company unless the target customer segment *perceives* the offer as meeting its needs best. So it's not enough to create the best experience and execute it well; it must also be communicated superbly. Everyone knows Wal-Mart has the lowest prices every day. In truth it doesn't always offer the lowest price on every item, but so many millions of consumers know and believe Wal-Mart's everyday-low-prices value proposition that the company brings in the most revenue of any company in the world.

Working through this very demanding process, Value Proposition Management entails six key steps, applied to each customer segment or subsegment:

Creation

1. *Synthesizing customer segment knowledge:* identifying the segment's needs, profitability, behavior, attitudes, and demographics, and evaluating how well the current value proposition meets the segment's needs versus competitors' value propositions.

2. *Hypothesis formulation:* developing possible new value propositions for the target customer segments and hypothesizing specifically how these new propositions would (a) bring in and retain more profitable customers and grow the profitable share of existing customers' total spend, and (b) improve the Customer Segment Value Creation Scorecard.

3. *Hypothesis testing and verification:* developing concrete experiments to (a) test specific hypotheses arising from possible new value propositions and (b) declare each hypothesis a winner, to be adopted on a larger scale, or a loser, to provide insight for changing the candidate value proposition.

Communication

4. *Communicating winning value propositions:* before moving to scale, developing messaging and media plans to educate target customer segments on how the new value propositions are better than those of competitors.

Execution

5. *Scaling successful experiments:* implementing the new value propositions in a big way, reflected in significant progress toward a sustained premium P/E for the segment.
6. *Knowledge accumulation:* tracking learning from the experiments and scaling, and then updating the customer segment knowledge inventory and beginning the cycle anew.

In this chapter we'll explore in detail the first three steps, which are the critically important preparation for action—the creation stage of VPM. We'll conclude with a discussion about the special value proposition challenges of value-destroying customers—those with negative economic profit. Then, in the following chapter, we'll discuss the remaining three steps, which guide managers' actions, where preparation turns into action, where the company "drives it to the ledger" and enhances the growth component of the premium P/E.

Most companies don't focus on the three stages of value proposition management today, though we believe most companies will have to begin doing so soon. Instead, many companies do bits and pieces of this process, often not realizing they're missing a tremendous opportunity to drive their share price.

For companies that are truly customer centered, VPM becomes the essential set of value-creating processes. The benefits of practicing

VPM over time are thus considerable. Yes, it will produce valuable customer knowledge, which will lead to ever more powerful new customer value propositions. But more important, practicing VPM over time will build a set of management practices that become part of the company's DNA, turning customer data into shareowner value continually, day after day. This is another reason that those who put customers at the center first will gain an ever increasing competitive advantage.

VPM does not have to be a complex process that is only for very large companies like Wal-Mart, IBM, or British Airways. A restaurant owner could adopt it with nothing more than a laptop computer, or even just pencil and paper. He could calculate customer profitability and then group customers into profitability deciles. He could analyze customer needs and define customer segments. He could create new value propositions for the different segments. For example, for the regular businesswoman customer who conducts important talks with clients, he could promise a quiet table and minimal interruptions. For the customer who likes specialty items—shad in the spring, soft-shell crabs in the summer, truffles in the fall—he could notify the customer when these foods become available and offer to reserve them for him. He could improve value propositions in these and a dozen other ways for clearly delineated customer segments and subsegments. So why don't more restaurant owners do it? Not for lack of technology, but for lack of mind-set; most businesspeople, in companies of every size, just don't yet think in these terms.

When rigorous, continuous measurement of value creation is part of the program, customer segment CEOs have their jobs on the line as they work to build premium P/E businesses. We know of many companies that have been deeply disappointed by the returns on their CRM investments, but we don't know of any companies that are following the VPM process and failing to grow revenue and reduce costs and invested capital.

The First Part of VPM: Creation

Because Steps 1, 2, and 3 of VPM are the foundation for the customer-centered increase in economic profit that will follow, they are critically important. As we discuss each of the six steps in detail in this chapter and the next, imagine yourself to be the CEO of the customer segment in your company that has the greatest potential to create a sustained premium P/E for your company. Jot down notes on how you might proceed through each of these steps.

VPM Step 1: Synthesizing Customer Segment Knowledge

In Chapter Six we discussed the customer-specific data needed to create and manage customer segment business units. We started with current profitability and future economic profit opportunity, then overlaid customer behavior to understand what drives profitability. We also incorporated demographics and attitudinal data to begin to better profile the customer—putting a face and name to the typical customer. Along with profitability, the most important element was characterization of customer needs—both cost and noncost needs.

How would this approach to synthesizing customer segment knowledge be applied to the airline example from earlier in the chapter? Looking across the population of customers, an airline would find that the top decile in profitability was heavily populated by frequent first-class fliers on the New York-London route. Looking at behavior indicates that this segment is profitable because its members travel often and pay the full first-class fare. Further analysis shows that these customers frequently depart from New York in the evening and return late the following afternoon on a regular flight or the Concorde. Often they don't stay in a hotel. Demographic analysis indicates that these travelers are senior business executives. Less frequent first-class travelers include vacationers, spouses, and children. All of this analysis leads to the profiling of this fabulously profitable segment as senior business executives who make frequent very short trips between New York and London.

Having profiled the customer segment, the airline's managers see clearly the segment's most important needs: saving time on departure and arrival and maximizing restful sleep on the plane. Supporting this intuition is extensive interviews with actual customers and other customer research.

The last portion of customer segment data to be inventoried is the current value propositions being offered this segment by the airline and its competitors. At the heart of this analysis is the search for ways to craft a total customer experience that meets key needs better than any competitor. An even greater opportunity lies in finding key unmet needs that no one is satisfying.

Collectively, all this data on the senior executive segment forms a sound knowledge base on which to build the search for a winning value proposition. This segment is highly profitable; the key is to retain current customers, win a larger share of their transatlantic flight business, and attract other customers who are flying with competitors.

In the information age, the amount of available customer data, like every other kind of data, is almost beyond imagining, a potential tidal wave of data that can easily overwhelm the unfocused user. It's a nice problem to have, but it's still a problem. Just because data is available doesn't mean a company is collecting it. Every company must decide what customer data to collect, how to collect it, and what to do with it. These are all large decisions.

Making the best use of customer data confers a greater competitive advantage than you may think. Every company has access to customer data. But of these, only some bother to collect it. Of these, only a few turn that data into useful customer knowledge. And of these, only a very few turn that knowledge into superior economic profit reflected in a premium P/E. Remember the Dismal Dozen we met in Chapter 1? There we see the problem exactly: Companies with access to unimaginable troves of customer data, yet each one dragging along with a consistently subpar P/E.

VPM Step 2: Hypothesis Formulation

"Everything starts with hypotheses," says Gaétane Lefebvre, vice president of strategic marketing research and analytics at RBC Financial Group, parent of Royal Bank. She means that for companies to create value from VPM, managers first have to *imagine* new, competitively superior value propositions that just might work.

While we've described a process that so far is highly rigorous, in many parts even mathematical, hypothesis formulation is creative, imaginative, sometimes intuitive, and hard to regiment or predict. This is what we have observed repeatedly in our interviews and examination of the most successful companies. In a customer-centered organization, the chiefs of the customer business units will have to bring together people from widely different disciplines—marketing, sales, research, finance, information technology, operations—who probably bring dissimilar mind-sets to work and may need practice working together (an important topic we will address in Chapter 9). But the more they can work together, the better, because new hypotheses arise out of personal experience and knowledge, so multiple heads are better than one. Deep knowledge of customers is essential, and it has to be in people's heads, not just in the company's computers. Lefebvre, whose department collects and analyzes vast amounts of customer data for RBC, loves just going through printouts of such data, sliced and diced in various ways, looking for insights.

Hypotheses based on customer information can range from modest to highly ambitious, but in every case they should be framed in explicit terms, with hypothesized results that are measurable and verifiable. Lowe's, the big chain of home-improvement centers, knew which customers had bought swingsets and decided to try a simple targeted mailing to those customers, promoting other items that might be of interest to the customer segment of families with three- to ten-year-old kids. This is the kind of interesting, novel idea that occurs in customer-centered companies; it probably wouldn't have happened in a traditionally organized company because it cuts across departments. That is, child-related products could come from throughout the store—electrical outlet covers from the electrical department, cabinet-locking devices from cabinetry, inflatable wading pools from the lawn and garden department. Each department has a chief, but no manager in the store would have been incentivized to think up this program. Promoting child-related merchandise was a new idea for home centers, and it happened to work.

In our airline example, understanding the needs and behavior of the very profitable New York-London senior executive might naturally lead one to hypothesize a new value proposition that would appeal to this segment. Given the very clear customer need for saving time and restful sleep, a customer segment team could well propose a new experience, including separate first-class express check-in and security clearance, a preflight express meal service in the first-class lounge so the time-pressed senior executive could maximize sleep time on the plane with minimum noise from the serving of in-flight meals, seats that recline into perfectly flat beds to provide restful sleep, and then a fast-track customs area in the UK airports to speed the executive on his or her way to meetings.

One final element of the experience is highly important: the fare. To implement the other elements of the new experience, the airline will have to incur additional costs and investments. Some, such as separate check-in and security, will not be major. Others, such as modifying the plane and installing new sleeper seats, will be. For this new value proposition to work for the airline as well as the customer, creating a mutually beneficial value exchange, this segment will have to pay a higher fare (perhaps by losing its deep corporate discounts).

In this example, the key hypotheses that the customer segment team will formulate revolve around the customer's response to each of the elements in the new experience and the holistic effect of all of the changes. Most especially, how will customers react to this value proposition compared to the competition's? Will the price increase stick? Will current customers be less prone to defect to competitors, and will they shift more of their travel budget to the new experience? Will satisfied customers persuade colleagues to try the new experience?

To answer each of these questions, hypotheses need to be specific and measurable. For example: The most popular flight times will be 100 percent sold out, with more than 90 percent of the customers coming from the target segment. Overall utilization will exceed 90 percent. The churn among the targeted customers will decline from 11 percent to 3 percent. Corporate discounts will decline from an average of $3,500 to $0. At least 95 percent of the senior executive segment will use the preflight meal service. Based on these hypotheses and many others, the customer segment CEO can prepare a new Customer Segment Value Creation Scorecard to evaluate this new value proposition versus the current one in terms of incremental economic profit and movement toward becoming a premium P/E business.

Sometimes a hypothesis can be elaborate. One of the customer segment chiefs at Royal Bank, Louise Mitchell, who was in charge of the Builders and Borrowers segment, had a big-idea hypothesis about mortgages for her segment. Like virtually all banks, Royal Bank ran a mortgage promotion during the home-buying season every spring. Like nearly all such promotions, it reminded consumers that Royal Bank offered mortgages, and it promoted the rates. But Royal Bank's research showed consumers assumed that all banks offered mortgages and that they were all about the same, which wasn't far from the truth.

So Mitchell decided to create a completely different approach, an initiative built not around mortgages but around the life event of buying a home—and not just any home, but a first home. Specifically, her hypothesis was that by creating a new value proposition that served the total needs of first-time home buyers, RBC could contribute to making her segment a premium P/E business in several ways. First-time home buyers have most of their financial lives ahead of them, so attracting them as customers holds the promise of a long-duration relationship with the prospect of significant future growth; on average they borrow larger amounts (meaning a larger investment opportunity for the bank) for longer mortgage terms (longer duration again) and are less rate sensitive than other home buyers (translating into a higher return on invested capital); all those factors combine into a terrific opportunity to create shareowner value. Mitchell understood all of this because her energies were focused entirely on understanding the Builders and Borrowers customer segment, the segment that includes first-time home buyers.

At this point we can observe a couple of generalizable facts. One is that RBC, like many companies, possessed vast information on all its customers; at most companies that information just sits there, but here it was used because of organizational structure, which created a segment leader who was powerfully incentivized to use the information. The second fact is that Mitchell is hypothesizing a new value proposition in exactly the way we have previously described in general—by discerning the critical homogeneous needs of a subsegment of customers, first-time home buyers.

Forming hypotheses based on customer interaction and data is at the very core of any successful customer-centered company. Every such company we have observed is constantly creating *lots* of hypotheses in the never-ending effort to create innovative competitive value propositions. It's in their blood. Turning out high volumes of hypotheses not only gives a company more shots at success but it also stretches people's minds and gives them experiences that make them better at it every day.

But some companies only hypothesize their hypotheses. They don't act on them. This leads us to Step 3.

VPM Step 3: Hypothesis Testing and Verification

Having crafted the new value proposition for the key subsegment, first-time home buyers, RBC next tested the hypothesis. Instead of running the usual advertising, the bank published a freestanding newspaper insert titled "First Home Buyers' Guide," filled with information and expert advice. It also used direct mail and e-mail. Through all these channels, the bank made a multipart offer that was quite novel: Besides giving you a mortgage, RBC would put $500 dollars into your savings account every year for five years and give you a free annual financial review for five years, free online banking for six months, free AOL for a year, and a no-fee Visa card.

This offer was intended to build relationships and create long-term customers. It will take years to say how well it succeeded in that effort, but the initial results were extremely positive. The bank increased its share of the total mortgage market and considerably increased its share among first-time home buyers (they were 50 percent of the overall market but 62 percent of RBC's new mortgages). The vast majority chose the longest, most profitable term for their mortgages.

This is another success that probably wouldn't have happened in a traditionally organized company. It required coordination among managers responsible for mortgages, savings accounts, financial advice, and marketing, among other things. None of them alone would have come up with the program as deployed; the marketers weren't at all sure about that freestanding insert, for example. But a customer-segment leader, accountable for the results, could be the powerful catalyst. The key, Mitchell says, was being customer centered, "looking through the customer lens." What does that mean? It means seeing things the way a customer does, not the way a banker does. A person doesn't take out a mortgage; a person buys a home. "See it that way," she says, "and the hypotheses jump right out."

Step 3 in VPM is crucial. It is where a company decides whether to reject a customer value proposition idea or move it to scale. If management gets this analysis wrong, shareowners can lose big. Wrongly rejecting a major competitive breakthrough or moving forward with a flawed premise can be highly damaging.

We've emphasized that hypotheses must be specific and measurable, and the main reason is to avoid such disasters. Only in this way can the financial case for a new value proposition be made clearly. In addition, learning increases exponentially when people are forced to hypothesize the specific outcome of an experiment; it avoids the all too easy rationalization of the outcome. It also forces the experimenter to think deeply through all the steps of the experiment and make assumptions along the way. The logic trail is often a key to understanding what the results are trying to tell us. Without that trail laid down before the experiment is conducted, it is too easy to look at any results and say, "I really knew that anyway."

The test of the hypothesis must be designed to ensure that exogenous factors don't cloud the outcome. Clear proof of a value proposition leads to action—charge! Disproof leads to learning—what did we have wrong about the customer segment definition, the relative weights of needs, or the appeal of a competitor's offer? But ambiguity leads to no action and no insight. Black-and-white results are both great, but gray is a disaster. To avoid results' being clouded by exogenous factors, such as bad weather, a dramatic shift in the economy, or major competitors merging, it is important to set up a control test. Whether customers are consumers or businesses, it is important to establish a test group and a control group as similar to one another as possible. If the test is of retail store customers, then virtually identical stores need to be found to ensure that the outcome is not being determined by an exogenous factor. We once helped a retailer in Southeast Asia develop and test value propositions. The economy was badly hit right in the middle of the experiment. The test store was up 2 percent versus our hypothesis of 14 percent, but the control stores, which were in similar neighborhoods with comparable customer mixes and traffic flows, were down over 30 percent. Had we not set up the controls properly, we might not have known that the new value proposition was actually a major success.

One of the best practice companies in creation and testing of customer value proposition hypotheses is Capital One Financial. Capital One tests tens of thousands of hypotheses every year. An example concerns customers who call up to say they're canceling their credit cards because they can get a better deal elsewhere. What's the best way to respond? Managers at the company came up with a number of hypotheses. One is that closing their accounts as requested makes the most sense; another is that they're really just angling for a better deal, and meeting the better offer they claim to have is smartest; a third possibility is to meet them somewhere in the middle, based on the calling customer's specific traits. Capital One tested each of these hypotheses on random samples of callers, then analyzed the results in light of the considerable data it already had on each customer. Based on this analysis, the company determined which response works best, based on the traits of the customer. Now when a customer service rep takes a call of this type, Capital One's computers instantly look at the caller's current and estimated future profitability, then judge his likely reaction to various offers, and tell the rep how to respond.

Capital One is an excellent example of how valuable it is to get different disciplines working together. The company formulates and tests over thirty thousand hypotheses every year; it's whole business model is built on this approach. Because the company must formulate and test so many hypotheses, it learned that it was essential to locate its information technology people physically next to its marketing people and its marketing people next to its risk analysis people. They must work together every day. It's interesting to note that this lesson would probably apply to many companies. As Capital One cofounder and CEO Rich Fairbank has often remarked, his company's "information-based strategy" could work in any number of industries.

* * *

Testing hypotheses along the various dimensions of the Customer Segment Value Creation Scorecard—trying different levels of spending on new customer acquisition, customer knowledge management, and customer relationship management, then measuring changes in share of wallet churn, return on invested capital, etc.—is a particularly powerful way of analyzing hypotheses and is the only way of rigorously refining them before deciding whether to move to scale. It's easier for some companies than for others. Big credit-card issuers like Capital One possess vast data about millions of customers and interact with thousands of them every day. They can and do test hundreds of different hypotheses, some only subtly different from one another, every day. At the opposite end of the spectrum, a company like Airbus may make only a few sales—of multibillion-dollar size—every year. In all cases, continually forming, testing, and refining hypotheses is the goal, and it's more achievable than managers tend to think. Even Airbus could do it, since in addition to planes it sells lots of spare parts every day, and it could also test hypotheses about the reactions of passengers to design changes or the reactions of airline executives to design, delivery, financing, and the many other elements of its value proposition.

Value-Destroying Customers: Fix, Close, or Sell Them

A particularly vexing problem that will arise in the first three steps of VPM is discovery of a segment or subsegment of customers that generate significant negative economic profit—decile 10. Organizing around customers can be a huge help for companies in handling this most difficult insight. Managers often resist this reality with particular vigor, and they may even be able to beat back efforts to address it. But when segment CEOs are accountable for segment performance, it's another story. All customer segment leaders confront this issue to varying degrees. In our experience, virtually every customer segment has its own decile 10 made up of unprofitable customers. On occasion, an entire segment of customers sharing homogeneous needs will yield negative economic profit. In such a situation, a large concentration of the corporate decile 10 customers often fall into this customer segment.

What to do about value destroyers? Your options—in terms that became popularized when Jack Welch winnowed GE's many businesses in the 1980s—are three: fix, close, or sell. Those choices have since been used by many managers in many companies to deal with problematic business units, but we've never seen this approach applied to customers. Yet it can be, and should be. The choice may not be easy and will probably require deep consideration. You may have to deal with tough issues of corporate culture and even internal accusations: The newly discovered fact that some customer segments are unprofitable will be regarded as evidence that someone did something wrong, and you'll have to get through the blame game before making progress. Your decisions will require thoughtful analysis, which becomes much easier in a business newly reorganized around customers, with most managers in new jobs and taking a new perspective.

Practically every manager's favorite alternative is to try to fix the unprofitable segments. Every company we've worked with has an organizational bias against saying goodbye to customers, even unprofitable ones. As Gail McGovern of Fidelity explains, "The word of mouth is bad, and who knows—you might terminate Bill Gates's grandmother." Executives at a number of companies have told us explicitly, "We believe every customer can be profitable." Common sense says that isn't true, but optimism is a virtue, and fixing unprofitable customers is clearly the best alternative if it's possible. After all, the customer is already in the door, and the company knows something about him or her. But trust us, some of your bottom decile customers are demons that can't be exorcised.

Making unprofitable customers profitable begins with a segment

CEO's applying the first three steps of VPM. Can she create a new customer experience that results in customers at least breaking even in economic profit terms? Her steps are the same: synthesizing customer segment knowledge, forming value proposition hypotheses, and testing and verifying these hypotheses. Exactly how best to do that depends on why a given customer or segment is unprofitable. Many reasons are possible:

    ⅄   Too early in life cycle. A customer may be too small to be profitable today but holds the potential of becoming a much larger, profitable customer in the future.

    ⅄   Insufficient volume. Some customers, while behaving normally, don't buy enough to cover the total costs, including capital costs, of serving them, and they're unlikely ever to buy much more than they're buying now. Still others buy less and do not even cover the direct variable costs of serving them.

    ⅄   Insufficient share of wallet. Other customers may be too small to be profitable but are doing significant business with direct competitors, so gaining more of their current business would make them profitable.

    ⅄   Bad behavior. Sometimes specific behavior turns an otherwise profitable customer unprofitable. For example, a customer of a home improvement store might buy profitable product bundles but still be unprofitable because she is constantly returning and exchanging items. Also, she may buy only on sale and then buy only the most discounted items.

Each reason for customer unprofitability requires a differently altered customer experience, and the appropriate changes will differ from company to company. For example, FedEx simply charges higher prices to customers whose behavior had previously made them unprofitable. Royal Bank changes the customer experience in a different way—changing the bank's activities to reduce the cost of serving

the customer. It can trace a check in one day for a profitable customer, but it will conduct a much less expensive three- to five-day
trace for an unprofitable and unpromising one. Of course in some
cases an unprofitable customer has unmet needs that the company
could satisfy very profitably. For example, a hotel guest who always
pays a low corporate room rate and orders a sandwich from room service (a money-losing activity) might be happy to spend a lot on food
and wine in the restaurant (a high-profit activity) if only it offered
what he wanted. An unprofitable bank customer might be willing to
move his highly profitable trading business to the bank if it offered
brokerage services. At the extreme, some unprofitable customers
could be not just profitable but hugely profitable if only the company
would understand and meet their needs—by applying steps 1, 2, and
3 of VPM.

The larger point is that VPM isn't about a company merely extracting the maximum number of dollars from each customer. It's
about creating the mutually beneficial value exchange we discussed
earlier. The company must create value propositions benefiting customers so much better than competitors that they'll provide the company with positive economic profit for years to come.

Fidelity Investments conducted extensive research into why some
of its customers were unprofitable. The trigger was their initial customer profitability analysis, which revealed that 10 percent of customers in their top segment, Private Access, all of whom maintained
at least $2 million of assets with the firm, were unprofitable. This re-
alization is what Gail McGovern, the executive then in charge of Fidelity's Personal Investments business, called "the big mind-boggling
moment of truth." When Fidelity dug deeper into what made some
customers unprofitable, it discovered that the main reason, accounting for just over half the losses attributable to unprofitable customers,
was excessive channel usage.

When a customer who does limited business with Fidelity calls
the call center too frequently, or gets on the phone with a branch of-

fice, or stops by an office to talk with a representative too often, the costs can easily outstrip any profits. Fidelity could identify specific customers who were unprofitable for this reason. So when such customers called, Fidelity's reps began teaching them how to use the company's lowest cost channels, its automated phone lines and Web site. Fidelity was subtly changing the customer experience in a way that was perceived initially by some customers as being slightly less satisfying, but cured the negative profit problem for Fidelity—moving the value exchange toward a better equilibrium. The cost differences are dramatic: Giving a customer a stock quote by phone from a rep costs Fidelity $13, while giving the customer a quote on-line costs 1¢. Fidelity also made its site friendlier, so customers would be more inclined to use it. These customers could still talk to service reps, but the phone system identified their calls and routed them into longer queues, so more profitable customers could be served more quickly—and the longer wait for the unprofitable customers would be a disincentive to call.

Fidelity couldn't lose. If these customers switched to lower-cost channels, they became profitable. If they didn't like the revised value proposition—slower service by phone, but better service on-line—and left, Fidelity was more profitable without them. In fact, however, 96 percent of these customers stayed, about the same retention rate as in the industry overall, and most of them switched to lower-cost channels. Over time customer satisfaction actually increased for the smaller customers as they learned how to save time and get faster service; that is, the company was meeting a previously unmet need. In addition, Fidelity's operating profit increased. The new value exchange equilibrium ended up being more satisfying for *both* the customers and Fidelity.

Fidelity's experience can be generalized to what happens when companies revise value propositions for unprofitable customers. If such customers decide to stay, that's an excellent development; under the new terms they are now profitable customers. And if the increased prices or modified services cause these customers to go elsewhere, that also is fine because they are no longer reducing the company's profits.[2] In fact, odds are strong they will end up patronizing a competitor who may not have conducted a customer profitability analysis and therefore won't realize he's just been saddled with a value destroyer.

In some cases companies find, despite their best efforts, that hypothesis after hypothesis on how to make the customer profitable fails when tested with real customers. These companies just cannot effectively revise the value proposition for certain unprofitable customers or customer segments. A retailer probably can't hire a bouncer to stand at the door and identify the value destroyers—the customers who buy only sale items, take lots of salespeople's time, make loads of returns even after the sales staff has done everything possible to get the size, fit, and color right, and pay their store credit card balances in full on the twenty-fifth day of the cycle. These are the demon customers for the retailer, and no known value proposition can create a mutually beneficial value exchange. But what can a company do about such customers? How can it close a customer segment? In a number of ways. The most common is simply to stop making any effort to attract those customers' business. FedEx, a pioneer in customer segmentation, lavishes lots of attention—mailings, phone calls, even personal visits—on profitable customers and those that could become profitable, but it targets no marketing whatsoever at customers who are unprofitable and unlikely to become so. Catalog retailers stop sending catalogs to customers who don't buy enough. By contrast, as a worst practice, consider some past tactics of AT&T and MCI WorldCom: At the height of the long-distance telephone wars, they were offering cash—up to $50—to any and all customers for switching carriers, with disastrous results. These offers attracted promiscuous customers who switched back and forth, collecting their cash incentive each time but never staying long enough for the company to earn back that acquisition cost. A smarter course would have been to identify customers who were likely to become profitable, loyal customers and ignore the rest.

Of course it's possible to close unprofitable customers in a more direct way. Fidelity Investments found that one of its customers, with a portfolio of only about $500,000, was asking for so much help and information that he was keeping three of its financial advisers busy virtually full-time. Eventually, reluctantly, and very politely, in this one case the company asked him to go elsewhere. A different company in a similar situation might have tried a different course, charging for customer counseling. Not managing your demon customers can have a huge cost. They may not be demons as individuals, but they are killing your stock. They are frustrating your most dedicated, hardest working employees, and they are robbing valuable resources from your most profitable, loyal customers. Do you as a leader have the courage to do what is right—or will you compromise in order not to lose a dollar of revenue?

What about the "sell" option? You can sell a business, but how can you sell an unprofitable customer segment? It isn't easy, but some companies can come close. As noted before, many retailers are pseudocustomer-centric because they treat individual stores or groups of stores as segments, designed, stocked, and run for the customers around them. These companies could sell stores that weren't creating shareowner value. Financial services firms sometimes structure business units around segments; think of gold and platinum credit cards. These units can be sold. The particular appeal of this course is that your competitors may not have done the segmentation and profitability analysis you have done, especially if you have carried the analysis to the point of calculating economic profitability and shareowner value creation. Your buyer therefore may not realize that he's buying an unprofitable customer segment, in which case your gain in his loss. In an increasingly competitive world, that outcome holds a lot of attraction. Or conversely, maybe your buyer's value proposition is crafted in such a way that it makes sense for your unprofitable segment; your buyer may be able to earn a profit on these customers. In that case, the transaction is a win-win, increasing the value of both companies. We'll talk more about this in Chapter 10.

We've achieved something significant: We've created winning value propositions. We know they're winners because we've verified, in tightly controlled tests, that they change customer behavior and improve economic profit. We understand why they do these things, because our hypotheses were highly specific and measurable. Now we're ready to communicate and execute these new value propositions on a broad scale. Doing so entails the final three steps of VPM. The result is major progress in creating or sustaining a premium P/E.

Driving It to the Ledger

Making Value Proposition Management Pay

"Driving it to the ledger" is a phrase they use at General Electric when they talk about implementing any new idea or initiative. It means just what it says: They want to push that new idea until they can see its effects in the financial results of the business unit where it's being tried. If they can't see clear, favorable financial results, then something's wrong. Either the idea isn't being implemented right or it's just a bad idea; they keep working on it until they make the idea pay or decide to throw it out. That relentless focus on results is a big reason the four major initiatives of CEO Jack Welch's twenty-year tenure—services, globalization, six-sigma quality, and digitization—each created billions of dollars of new value for GE's shareowners. It's also why one of the first managerial tools we introduced here was the Customer Segment Value Creation Scorecard.

Becoming customer centered holds more potential for value creation than any of those four big ideas.[1] Realizing that potential requires an unwavering insistence on driving it to the ledger—not being satisfied until you can see the payoff on the Customer Segment Value Creation Scorecard. The second part of VPM is where the payoff arrives.

The first stage of VPM, you'll recall, consists of three steps: synthesizing customer segment knowledge, hypothesis formulation, and hypothesis testing and verification. The part of VPM we discuss in this chapter consists of the three remaining steps:

4. Communicating winning value propositions
5. Scaling successful experiments
6. Knowledge accumulation

The first part of VPM is preparation. Now we're ready for action.

VPM Step 4: Communicating Winning Value Propositions

We've all had the occasional experience at a restaurant, hotel, or store where we walked out incredulous at how terrific it was. Later we raved to friends and family about every detail. More often than not it was unexpected, which made our discovery that much more notable. Maybe you've experienced the same thing in your life as a businessperson—encountered a supplier that really saved you when you had a crisis or worked around the clock to help you win a new, highly profitable account. A critical challenge for that supplier and for every business with a fabulous value proposition is to get the message out to the right target customer segment. Then customers will seek out the exceptional experience rather than discover it by accident.

Returning to our airline example begun in the previous chapter, the customer segment chief has just learned that the new customer experience his team created—the candidate for a new value proposition—is winning rave reviews in experiments. All of the specific, quantifiable metrics we discussed in the previous chapter are being met or exceeded. The Customer Segment Valuation Scorecard shows that a successful launch and execution of this value proposition would generate an obscene increase in economic profit and indicate a great opportunity to improve the segment's intrinsic P/E. Now if the segment decides to scale the experiment, how should it communicate the message?

The first part of step 4 is targeting the right audience for the message. Identifying that audience begins with the work the airline has already done to segment and subsegment the customer pool. But as we will discuss in the context of scaling successful experiments, target subsegments can often be expanded to include a somewhat broader population.

In targeting the message, one must distinguish between the individual who will experience the new value proposition and two other, possibly important, related groups. First, the purchaser can often be different from the user. This can be critically important if the purchaser thinks only about price. A trucking company might consider buying a new model truck that costs more but gets excellent fuel economy and spends less time in the shop. Corporate purchasing may be looking only at the vehicle's initial price and not its fuel cost and down time, ignoring the correct perspective of total life cycle cost. Second, influencers may need to understand the value proposition— spouses play a key role in some purchase decisions, for example. The communication must take account of these related groups, which may focus on different elements of the value proposition.

The second part of step 4, after targeting the right audience, is getting the message right. When Royal Bank of Canada targeted first-time home buyers, it understood the importance of making customers aware of the importance of certain needs. Those buyers sort of knew that price or rate wasn't the most important issue for them, but RBC clearly communicated what was: getting help going through the scary and seemingly complex process of buying a home for the first time.

This is likely the biggest financial decision these customers have ever made. Knowing that they are doing the right thing and will not regret the decision later is their most important need. Later in life, when they refinance or buy a second house, this need will become less important, and the customer most likely will move into a new segment with a different value proposition. The key here is to get your customers focused on their most important needs and then demonstrate how the complete experience you are offering is tailored to them and will meet their needs better than the competition.

In our experience, corporate buyers often exhibit an odd tendency to misidentify their own most important needs when choosing suppliers. This is particularly common when the company buying the product or service is itself not customer centered. Too often it will focus on just price, not understanding the impact of the purchase decision on its own customers. We've seen companies push very hard to save a few dollars in procurement and then lose a highly profitable customer because their miserly purchasing forced them to offer an inferior value proposition. A truly customer-centered supplier understands its customers' economics and in particular its customers' customers well enough to identify ways of increasing its customers' economic profit.

The third part of communicating the winning value proposition is making sure that the message doesn't confuse the customer because of overall brand perception or other marketing communications. One of the masters of customer segmentation and value proposition creation is Southwest Airlines. Their target customer segment may surprise you: It is frequent, short-haul business travelers. Their key needs are frequent flights and on-time performance. Since the corporate "purchaser" is probably in procurement, his need is for low prices. But if employees scream about inconvenient schedules and late arrivals that blow their meetings, intracompany fist fights are not far off. Southwest has mastered the sweet-spot value proposition, excelling at frequency of flights, on-time performance, and low price. Recently the airline has expanded into longer trips and may find it difficult to meet customer expectations of flight frequency and on-time performance. The company runs the risk of damaging its brand—customers may get confused about what needs Southwest is really trying to meet and how well it's doing.

VPM Step 5: Scaling Successful Initiatives

Here's a straightforward example of a hypothesis that worked and was worthy of scaling to company-wide use. Michael Walker, who's in charge of Royal Bank's Wealth Preservers customer segment, noticed a potentially large opportunity. Wealth Preservers are the bank's oldest, richest customers. Though only one of the bank's customer segments, accounting for 20 percent of customers, they account for two-thirds of the bank's deposits. Royal Bank has been highly successful in basing hypotheses on customers' life events, and for many Wealth Preservers the next big life event will be the last one.

When Wealth Preservers pass away, their abundant assets typically get transferred to a younger generation. A lot of money is involved: Over 80,000 of the bank's customers die each year, transferring $4 billion of assets held in the bank. But most of that money—70 percent—was not staying with the bank, either because it was being transferred to heirs who were not customers or because the heirs who were customers were putting it elsewhere.

Walker's hypothesis was that if Royal Bank could improve the experience of settling the estates of deceased customers, it could achieve two important results: keeping more of those assets, and building better relationships with the heirs, who were typically in the Builders and Borrowers segment—the bank's most profitable segment, just ahead of Wealth Preservers. So, in a test with a sample of customers, the bank thoroughly revised the value proposition it offers current and potential customers who have to settle estates. This revised value proposition introduced new customer experiences and altered others. The estate settlement process can involve tons of paperwork, so the bank made it easier and more efficient. Since settling an estate is a chore most people don't know much about, the bank built a new financial advice and planning program so it could offer specific help to heirs who had probably never faced this situation before. Royal Bank employees got advice on dealing with bereaved heirs. It improved its related back-end processes so they happened faster and with less hassle.

The experiment was a clear success. Instead of keeping just 30 percent of deceased customers' assets, as before, the bank kept 50 percent. And because it was making the heirs happy with better care, advice, and operations, it also increased new deposits 25 percent, mostly from highly profitable customers. Extrapolating from the sample, the bank calculated that applying this initiative nationally would translate into about $1.5 billion of net incremental balances each year. Because Royal Bank already was calculating the economic profit for its Wealth Preserver customers, it could easily translate the results of the experiment into specific dollar increases in economic profit and shareowner value creation. In other words: This value proposition experiment is a winner—communicate it and roll it out.

Which the bank did, relatively easily. It distributed the new customer care and advice programs to the branches and financial planners through existing channels, and it scaled up the improved back-end processes at headquarters in Toronto. The rollout was nontraumatic, and in short order the program was in place company-wide and well on its way to creating the new economic profit that was forecast in the scale plan.

This story is encouraging but not typical. Most companies, no matter how they're organized and no matter what their culture, can test a customer-centered hypothesis by doing it on a small scale and having a manager walk the changes through every department or territory involved. But when it's time to scale up, that approach won't work. As we've observed, customer-centered initiatives almost always cut across boundaries in a traditionally organized company. They often require departments that rarely work together to work together; these initiatives may need to move authority to new places.

It's a recipe for organizational paralysis unless the company is truly customer-centered. Royal Bank is, which is why it could scale up its estate settlement initiative easily and quickly. Think of what was involved: new processes for employees in the branch network and for the financial planners, new materials for these employees, new processes in the back office, all coordinated across a company with ten million customers. At Royal Bank these changes were part of everyday business processes. Could a traditionally organized bank implement them? Yes, in theory. But think about the bank we met at the beginning of this book, the Bank of Outer Mongolia, whose mortgage department had never heard of—and didn't care much about—one of the bank's best customers. Implementing a company-wide, cross-departmental, customer-centered initiative in that outfit would be like rolling a boulder up a mountain.

The RBC example highlights two key principles that are critical in scaling any new value proposition hypothesis:

Accountability

Customer-centered hypotheses are a new breed of cat in most organizations. They require people throughout the company to imagine doing new things in new ways. Some people in the organization will find certain hypotheses threatening or baffling or maybe just wrongheaded, even before they've been tested. Practically every organization is full of forces that are ready to shoot a hypothesis down the minute it gets off the ground. Perhaps worse, most organizations have plenty of people who, seeing danger in a new approach to things, will say, "It's not my job." And given the way many companies operate, you can't necessarily blame those people.

That's why someone must be explicitly accountable for formulating hypotheses and for driving their implementation to achieve results, which will be rigorously evaluated based on their ability to increase economic profit and contribute to a premium P/E. This may seem self-evident, but many companies that think they're gung-ho users of customer knowledge in fact assign responsibility for it to the marketing department or to the sales operation. That won't work because people in those areas can't be held accountable for the total customer; after all, they may not have any say over fulfillment of the order, or billing, or after-sales service, or some other important part of the customer experience. What's more, they may not have access to—and probably won't have the incentive to use—the full trove of customer data the company may possess or be able to get. Hey, if I'm just marketing the product, I'm not going to worry about responding to service complaints in ways that maximize each customer's economic profit. That's too far removed from what I'm evaluated on and getting paid for, and it would just use time and money in ways that won't help me reach my incentive goals.

We've said before that total customer accountability is key, and now the reasons are becoming clearer. In every example cited and every case we know of, when value proposition improvements or reinventions pay off they inevitably cut across the boundaries separating traditional departments or territories or functions. Only managers who are accountable for total economic profit from specific customers or segments—that is, whose heads will be on the block if the results aren't driven to the ledger—will cross these boundaries and make things happen.

Alignment

This is accountability's inseparable companion. What we've seen in every example so far is true in general: In successful customer-centered initiatives, disparate parts of the organization must work together. They must have aligned goals and objectives so everyone is pulling in the same direction, the direction of creating greater economic profit from customers. It would be tempting to use the term authority rather than alignment here: It seems logical that in order to get everyone pulling together, the customer segment chiefs must have the authority to make them do so. And it's true that at some companies, such as Fidelity, the segment chiefs have that authority explicitly. But at other highly successful customer-centric organizations, such as Royal Bank, they don't. Instead, these organizations rely on what we might call a cultural imperative to align the many parts of the company. Through the way they hire, develop, incentivize, and evaluate employees, plus the values conveyed from top management, these companies get their various departments and territories to behave in alignment with the company's customer-centered way of operating.

Frankly we're skeptical when companies claim they can get managers to operate for the greater good strictly as a result of a corporate culture. For the vast majority of companies, clear reporting relationships always seem a more reliable mechanism, and that approach certainly works. Still, we can't ignore the evidence. That's why we say whether you achieve the goal through lines of explicit authority or in some other way, alignment of all parts of the company toward creating shareowner value from customers is key.

Evaluation of initiatives—that is, calculating how initiatives increase or decrease a company's economic profit—is a process we've been through in detail already. How to do it is clear whether it's testing a value proposition hypothesis or scaling up a successful experiment. But in doing it, companies show a dispiriting tendency to forget a couple of important principles:

First, carrying the analysis all the way to economic profit and a relative P/E is vital. In most companies the deeply entrenched tradition is to evaluate initiatives on some other criterion: gross margin, market share, customer satisfaction, customer retention, or any of a dozen other measures. Those measures may be important, but ultimately they aren't good enough because you can increase every one of them in ways that destroy shareowner value. You can build gross margin by making capital investments that reduce labor costs; it works because the capital costs aren't included in gross margin. You can buy market share with price cuts. You can increase customer satisfaction and retention through all sorts of giveaways to the customer that will cost the company dearly. Only by looking at customer economic profit and a contribution to a premium P/E can one make a sound judgment about the success of an initiative—and one *can* calculate the impact on economic profit and relative P/E. The focus of economic profit is short term while that of the relative P/E is long term, as the latter depends on the size of future investment opportunities and the sustainability of returns on invested capital in excess of capital costs. The process will require making some assumptions, as noted in previous chapters, but as a company repeats the process over time it will accumulate data that will turn those assumptions (about customer duration, for example, or capital allocation) into numbers used with ever greater confidence. And even when the calculation has to be based on assumptions or estimates, it's still the right calculation to be making. As the saying goes, it's better to be approximately right than precisely wrong.

Second, it's important to remember that the evaluation of any initiative is really just an evaluation of the first try. We don't know of any hypothesis, no matter how successful it was when implemented, that was ever repeated or scaled in exactly the same way in which it was originally tried. Everyone learns from experience. Some hypotheses will appear on evaluation to be promising but not obvious home runs. In these cases it may be worth refining the hypothesis using a sensitivity analysis: I'd like to increase this project's economic profit from X to Y; based on experience, I think I see an opportunity to in-crease return on invested capital by spending more on pro-active cross-selling of services and intellectual property to target customers; what combinations of increased spending and higher return would give me the extra value I'm looking for? In this way some hypotheses can be retried and turned into big winners (or discarded as hopeless mediocrities) before a decision is made on whether to expand them.

A final note on scaling successful experiments to drive economic profit. In Chapter 6 we introduced the Segmentation Matrix, on which customer segments and subsegments can be plotted on one axis reflecting degree of homogeneity of needs and on another axis show-ing profitability. The ideal segment possesses highly homogeneous needs and offers great profitability. The advantage of homogeneous needs is obvious: This trait makes it easier to find one or two primary needs that can drive the search for a winning value proposition. The segment of senior executive fliers between New York and London is a useful example.

Unfortunately, as one subsegments to find greater homogeneity, the subsegment's financial potential often declines with its size. De-spite this phenomenon, we have often found it useful to tilt for homo-geneity at the expense of financial opportunity. Doing so produces a clearer picture of the customer and often yields much more powerful and focused value propositions. The good news is that once a winning value proposition is developed for a subsegment of customers, we typ-ically find that the subsegment's definition can be broadened in a way that yields more profit. Example: The senior executives flying be-tween New York and London are a very small subsegment of cus-tomers, but focusing on their needs stimulated a strikingly clear value proposition. An airline can then apply that same value proposition, or simple variations involving certain elements of the overall customer experience, to other transatlantic and then transoceanic flights. In addition, some of the insights gained can probably be applied in creating value propositions for other segments flying in business class.

VMP Step 6: Knowledge Accumulation

Nothing's forever, and even the most successful initiatives need to be revised or reinvented over time. Competitors improve their value propositions, consumer tastes change, the economy booms or busts, customers get older—these and many other shifts in the environment can turn a winning idea into a loser. That's life for every company, no matter what its business model.

Every business process includes a feedback loop, and VPM is no different. In this case it's particularly important because it yields the most valuable benefit of the entire process, the creation and growth of customer knowledge as a significant corporate asset. By continually gathering data, analyzing it, forming hypotheses, testing them, and scaling the winners, a company is learning. That learning makes the next iteration of the cycle more effective. Over and over the process is repeated, each time creating more and better customer knowledge. Codifying this learning and disseminating it to the appropriate customer business units provides an ever increasing competitive advantage.

Getting maximum success from this step means more than just tracking bottom-line results. Specifically, making VPM most successful requires keeping track of all the elements of being truly customer centered.

> ⅄ **Are your customer segments still defined optimally?**
> Are you uncovering new customer needs or perhaps weighting their importance differently, and is that creating the basis of new segments or subsegments? Has any segment become so large or so broad that it should be subdivided? If you think not, are you sure? Companies consistently tend to make seg-

ments too large rather than too small. Recall Dell's experience over many years of finding that sales increased every time it subdivided a customer segment. Have your segments blurred together too much?

∀ **Are you updating your analysis of profitability deciles?**

Watching changes in the distribution and average profit levels of the deciles at the corporate and customer segment levels can be particularly enlightening. Are you making significant progress on reducing decile 10 losses and growing decile 1 and 2 profits? Are customers in deciles 3 and 4 starting to achieve profit levels previously realized by decile 2? Customer segment CEOs should be working hard on their own profit decile charts, and the collective efforts of all the segments should be showing up at the corporate level.

∀ **Are you developing and testing new value propositions?**

If not, it may be time for customer business unit chiefs to redirect their efforts or get some new thinking on the case. The opportunities for refining and reinventing customer experiences are unlimited.

∀ **Are the current components of the Customer Segment Value Creation Scorecard moving in the right direction?**

The details of the Scorecard—costs, returns, invested capital, customer gains and losses—provide an early warning system that can indicate trouble before it significantly affects economic profit.

∀ **Are the other elements of intrinsic P/E improving, holding steady, or deteriorating?**

The Scorecard tells you the best estimates of future return on invested capital and the size of investment opportunities. You'll also want to track the duration of customer relationships and the cost of the capital. Since these are the ultimate determinants of a premium P/E, each customer business unit is accountable for monitoring and delivering them.

The six steps of Value Proposition Management are the key components of creating shareowner value from customers. They work, but only if an organization is capable of putting them to work. The nuts and bolts of making that happen, of making an enterprise truly customer centered, is the topic we take up next.

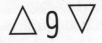

△ 9 ▽

Becoming Truly Customer Centered

The Nuts and Bolts of Making It Happen in Your Organization

Before a company can make the very challenging change to a customer-centered organizational structure, with all its many advantages, it must possess certain foundation stones. These basic traits are common to all organizations that have made this transformation. In addition, the organization's leaders have to make the case for action; in most companies the change will be significant, and the argument for it must be compelling. Then and only then can leaders make the transformation happen, getting enthusiastic acceptance throughout the organization on the three key fronts—technical, political, and cultural—and to all key constituencies. This chapter is about that process: placing the foundation stones, making the argument for action, and executing the transformation.

The Foundation Stones

We've observed six key traits that characterize organizations fully prepared to become truly customer centered:

Mind-set

This is the first and most important stone in the foundation. It's the word we hear more than any other when we talk to managers in companies that are truly customer centered and those that are struggling to become so. It means that everyone in the company is comfortable with the idea of driving shareowner value by measuring and managing customer segments through VPM. Two key aspects of this are recognizing that not all customers are created equal and that this insight must drive resource allocation. While simple, those precepts represent a huge change at most companies. But until they become the corporate mind-set, the transformation effort can't succeed.

Making that big shift is rarely easy, but it's easier if the organization is facing crisis—or, as Bell South CFO Ron Dykes says in a phrase we like, "if your hair is on fire." If it isn't, then the situation demands an extra dose of leadership. At Royal Bank, which was not facing a crisis, Vice Chairman Jim Rager made clear that the change in mind-set was total and immediate, and was expected to produce big results. Dell Computer was doing fine at a point when it had categorized its individual customers into seven segments but hadn't segmented its business customers at all. To make the next step of segmenting business customers, "Michael Dell orchestrated a shift in our mind-set," says former CFO Tom Meredith.

When we say mind-set comes first, we're saying explicitly that it's more important than technology; many people make the mistake of thinking the opposite must be true. But think of all the dot-coms that possessed every advantage in being customer-centered if they had wanted to be. They were starting with a clean slate—no corporate politics or power structures to take apart. No old computer systems to throw out or adapt. Since their businesses were online, and thus able to collect data about every customer easily and cheaply and target high-value ones, these companies were positioned better than any in history to be customer centered. But did they do it? Admittedly this is mostly a forensic exercise, but based on the evidence available, it seems most dot-coms were not truly customer-centered. They had everything but the mind-set. On the other hand, the few survivors include perhaps the most relentlessly customer-centered dot-com of them all, eBay.

Preliminary data

The full power of organizing around customers won't be apparent until a company has done it, but few companies will go ahead with such a momentous change before they've seen hard evidence that it can work for them. Thus it's necessary to assemble data showing that in some part of the company, this change really has worked.

One food retailing company we worked with was better prepared than most. It was able to calculate economic profit for its entire business and for all its products. It also had crunched the data for two customer models. One was a customer segmentation model based on lifestyles, and the other was a financial model based on gross margin dollars. The bad news was that the two segmentation models were not aligned and were sitting on different databases. Thus the company didn't have the all-important data showing economic profitability of the lifestyle-based segments. When it took the critical final step of merging its two segmentation models, the senior leaders were, of course, astonished by the revelation of who was and wasn't economically profitable. This new information enabled the company to refine its value propositions in ways that increased economic profit significantly.

Even without the advantages this company had, it is far simpler and faster to gather such information than most managers suspect. We have participated in projects that took only sixty days to show, on the basis of sample data, that top management's assumptions about the company's most and least profitable customers were radically wrong. In companies with large customers, it isn't even necessary to rely on sample data; a profitability analysis of just a few customers will almost always shock the company's managers. Regardless of how they're generated, some kind of preliminary results are needed to get the ball rolling. Once it starts rolling, it's hard to stop; the more managers learn, the more they want to know.

Customer-centered people

We agree with the old principle that you hire for attitude and train for skills. If a company is going to be truly customer-centered, it needs employees who are genuinely, completely comfortable with the notion of customers at the center of everything. That doesn't mean every employee has to be outgoing and good looking; not everyone is on the front lines. But it means no employee can be uncomfortable with the notion that not all customers are created equal, so some should be treated differently from others based on needs and profit potential—treated differently, not badly! No employee can resent, even a little, the mantra that customers are the source of all good things for the company. You'd be surprised—or maybe you wouldn't be—by how many employees regard customers as a pain in the neck and wish they'd just go away.

A service culture

This foundation stone is similar to but not quite the same as the previous one. We want to be clear that organizing around customers is not the same as offering great customer service. Much has been written about service, but we're talking about something more radical, about changing how a company measures and manages its most basic activities. Nonetheless, it's virtually impossible for a company to reorganize itself around customers unless it has a strong service culture. Without it, the organization just won't accept the basic primacy of customers. And of course a central element of the most powerful value propositions at many of the most successful customer-centered firms is a great service experience—appropriate for the customer's profit potential—at every touch point with the organization. In making this happen, the buck stops with the customer segment CEO.

Explicit recognition of customer segment dynamics

One of the great advantages of organizing around customers is that it blows up the product silos that stand in the way of realizing a premium P/E at most companies. As we've shown many times, a company composed of product organizations will displease valuable customers while wasting resources on less valuable ones—all in the name of maximizing product profitability (and even this, as we've seen, is often miscalculated because companies ignore operating and capital costs). But it's important to recognize that organizing around customers, while addressing this problem, has the potential to create a different problem. Product silos could simply be replaced with customer silos. Each customer segment manager could focus solely on maximizing the financial performance of his segment, ignoring a crucial reality: Customers often move from one segment to another. At Dell, for example, a customer in the small- and medium-sized business segment could grow into a customer of the large business segment. That's great news for Dell, even though it means the manager of the small- and medium-sized business segment loses a customer. So it's in Dell's interest for that segment manager to pass that customer along to the next segment, rather than fight to keep him. After all, if a segment manager insists on clinging to customers whose needs can no longer be served best in that segment, those customers will be inappropriately served, receiving value propositions that aren't optimal for them, and customer economic profit won't get maximized.

The general principle is that customers migrate among segments (or out of the company) over their lives as a result of evolving needs, a shifting competitive environment, and macroeconomic change. That tendency is clearest at a financial services firm, where retail customers often start out small, grow as they become more financially successful, and eventually die and pass on their wealth, with their various needs and profitability levels changing along the way. The customer life cycle will unfold differently in other businesses; if you sell to a megacompany like General Motors or Johnson & Johnson, the relationship may last many decades. But in any business, customers will fall naturally into different customer segments over the years. So it's vital that a customer-centered company understand and face the reality of the customer life cycle. That may mean taking steps as simple as compensating managers partly on the basis of all the segments' or the whole company's success, and partly on their own segment's success. Fidelity and Royal Bank, in businesses with fairly clear and predictable customer life cycles, both follow this policy, which at least encourages managers to cooperate and hand off customers as appropriate. Again, culture is also important. At a company where managers learn to get ahead by stabbing each other in the back, incentives will accomplish only so much. The fact of central importance is that managers must find a way to work together so customer segment dynamics increase the value of the whole firm rather than become a source of conflict, wasted resources, and value destruction.

Committed leadership

Some important corporate changes bubble up from the bottom. This isn't one of them. We don't know of a company that has become truly customer centered, including being organized around customers, without complete commitment from top leadership, and we wouldn't expect the facts to be otherwise. This is a major transformation. The organization won't believe it's real—won't begin the crucial shift in mind-set—unless the top dogs make it their own, betting their careers and their equity in the company on the success of the transformation.

The Argument for Action

A company in transformation needs more than these foundation stones. The CEO and senior team must make the case for action, and they must make it to all major constituencies: customers, the board, investors, and employees (and perhaps other important stakeholders, such as suppliers, regulators, and the community). To be most persuasive, this argument must be based on shareowner value, which is the basis of the company's ability to serve not just investors but also customers and employees.

Your company either has a premium P/E or it doesn't, two cases that cover all possibilities and demand action no matter what:

> ▼ If the P/E is subpar, then part of the leader's job is to spell out in detail the unpleasant future that awaits the company and everyone in it if the P/E remains less than great while also describing the phenomenal opportunities for everyone if the company can create and sustain a premium P/E. Your company today is simply not a place where investors prefer to park their capital. That means you'll fall behind your competitors in trying to attract top talent with stock ownership, in funding new initiatives for thrilling existing customers and attracting new ones, and in acquiring other companies that have talent, customers, and market share that you'd like. Your company's failure on all these dimensions will probably drive your P/E multiple even lower, making these problems worse, and the vicious circle will keep spiraling down toward cutbacks, layoffs, and

endless other kinds of corporate misery. Your company's current way of doing business—a product focus, perhaps, functional silos, inability to measure or manage customer profitability—is what got you here, and continuing on that course is not going to produce the dramatic change needed to transform your lousy P/E into a premium P/E.

∀   If the company already has a premium P/E, then the case for action is almost equally urgent. Remember the multiplier effect we discussed in Chapter 4? It's wonderful to be up there with a high multiple, but you're standing on a narrow pinnacle with steep slopes on every side. One slip—such as a failure to meet earnings expectations—and your share price will plunge because investors will apply a lower multiple to your lower earnings. That's the multiplier effect, and, as we've mentioned, it can wipe out significant amounts of value in the blink of an eye, as it has for many high fliers such as AOL, Oxford Health Plans, and Procter & Gamble.

But, employees and directors may reasonably ask, if our present way of doing business got us to this exalted state, why change? If it ain't broke, why fix it? The answer is that your premium P/E is guaranteed to be attracting lots of competition; other companies want a piece of the stupendous value you're creating. Continuing on your present course is not going to keep you ahead of that hungry pack. And by the way, no matter what your competitors are doing, your company is not immune to a nasty tendency that statisticians call regression to the mean. When performance jumps way above average—whether it's the economy's, a company's, a stock picker's, a designated hitter's, or anyone else's—it tends to fall back toward average eventually. You're fighting not only competitors but also what seems to be the law of gravity.

The only way to avoid a value meltdown is to keep innovating your value proposition and adopt a new approach to your business that puts you even further ahead of your existing and potential competitors. As we have said before, becoming customer-centered offers clear first-mover advantages and creates strengths that are extremely difficult for competitors to imitate. So while you may have a premium P/E now, are you going to wait for competitors to see the compelling advantages of becoming truly customer-centered and knock down your premium P/E? Or are you going to make the needed changes and beat them to the punch?

The Three Dimensions in Which a Company Must Change

After setting out such a shareowner value-based argument for action, a company intent on becoming truly customer-centered must make changes simultaneously along a number of dimensions. Our good friend and colleague Noel M. Tichy, professor at the University of Michigan Business School and former chief of General Electric's Crotonville Leadership Development Center, has identified these critical dimensions as technical, political, and cultural.[1] Corporate transformation won't happen until a company changes itself fundamentally in all three areas. We can describe how the transformation to customer-centricity takes place along these dimensions:

Technical

The technical aspect means the strategy and how it gets executed. It includes setting the company's financial goals, customer profitability, understanding behavior and needs, determining customer segments, and then implementing VPM. This includes what gets measured, which processes are performed, and how. It's the nuts and bolts of operations and staff support. In fact, it is much of what we've discussed in previous chapters. In particular, it involves the specific aspects of the organizational change.

It's important to integrate the new organizational structure relentlessly into business planning processes. That means every process—budgeting, for starters, and not just at the corporate level, at every level. Also information technology, facilities management, marketing, public relations, human resources, and every other part of the organization—all will need to adapt to the reality of truly putting customers at the center. The leadership will want to know—must demand to know—how every area of the business is planning for the change. That's necessary in order to make the change happen and to make clear that it is not a top-management flavor of the month.

Many companies have found it's useful to create internal experts and champions for the change. For managers and other employees, making any significant change is much more than just being told to do it; it's also learning how to do it. Propagating the change by having employees teach other employees, who will in turn teach others, offers many advantages. It's highly efficient; if one trained employee can teach ten more, each of whom can teach ten more, the most important elements of the change spread through the organization like kudzu. People respond better to teaching from a coworker than from an outsider. They also learn better—you learn best when you know you're going to have to teach this material to someone else.

The internal technical changes required when organizing around customers can be summarized as follows:

From	To
Tracking product P&L	Tracking customer P&L
Product development	Customer needs assessment
Developing product strategy	Developing customer value propositions

Calculating product net present value	Calculating customer net present value
Product sales	Relationship management
Managing product life cycle	Managing customer life cycle
Running product business reviews	Running customer business reviews

Political

In a company, the political realm is all about power. Who gets hired and who gets fired? Who gets to make key decisions? Who gets rewarded and how well? Pushing change on the political front means changing the answer to the question: How do I get promoted around here?

Changing a company's organizational structure causes huge power shifts. There are winners and losers. For example, no matter how strongly we emphasize the importance of product managers, there's no escaping the fact that in a customer-centered company they are subsidiary to the segment managers. It must be so. As a practical matter someone has to be in charge, if only to resolve the inevitable conflicts. The flip side is that putting one group of managers clearly in charge helps eliminate duplication of effort—it may not be necessary for product and segment organizations to conduct separate studies of a new market, for example.

To put it as bluntly as possible: In product-centered companies the product managers are kings; in customer-centered companies they are not. Similarly in function- and territory-centered companies, becoming customer centric represents a major shift in power. That simple fact is probably the largest obstacle to companies' making the change. The ability to overcome the obstacle is therefore a defining test of leadership at the top.

The experience of Royal Bank is instructive. Vice Chairman Jim

Rager made the change from a product-centered to a customer-centered organization clearly and cleanly. Everyone's importance was respected, but there was no double-talk about everyone's roles being the same as they used to be; it was absolutely clear that a new group of executives were now at the top of the food chain. To break the inevitable tension with a laugh, product managers would sometimes exaggeratedly bow down to the new segment chiefs. But the fact is that some product managers and regional heads just weren't happy in their new roles, and they left the bank. That was not a cause for concern, nor should it have been. It was an inescapable part of the process.

Actions speak louder than words, and nothing shouts "We mean it" like pay and advancement. Thus it's critical to align decision making, compensation, and promotion practices with the shift to customer centricity. Conversely, you can make all the ringing declarations you like about the importance of organizing around customers, and if compensation and promotion practices don't change, the organization quite rationally ignores all the noise. It's just human nature that people don't make big changes in their lives, including their work lives, unless doing so affects them positively in a very direct way, and failing to make these changes affects them negatively.

It's important to reward employees not just for behavior but for results. Yes, it's vital that they behave in a customer-centric way, but unless such activity increases economic profit, it's pointless. Employees must be rewarded for driving it to the ledger: It's not enough for those organizing the company around customers simply to show that they're taking the steps. They must also show that the change is doing good things for the drivers of a premium P/E, spread, duration, and investment size. That sounds obvious, but you'd be amazed how many companies gauge their success at transformation by whether they've carried out designated activities, not by whether they've achieved designated results.

In a company that's becoming truly customer centered, the political shift can be summarized as follows:

From	To
Strategy driven by product organization	Strategy driven by customer segment CEOs
Products and territories are dominant in resource allocation.	Customer segments are dominant in resource allocation.
Function heads or product business unit heads are best compensated.	Best-performing customer segment heads are best compensated.
Incentives reward product profitability.	Incentives reward customer profitability.
CEO successor comes from functional areas or product business units.	CEO successor comes from customer business units.

Cultural

Ultimately, putting customers at the center is more than a matter of corporate organization and management. It's a matter of corporate culture. Every company that has made the change or that has tried to do so realizes this.

What is culture? It is simply the corporate values that lead people to do what they'd do when no one is telling them what to do. In the modern organization, with its reduced hierarchies and empowered workers, that means what most people are doing most of the time. Since virtually none of us has been brought up through an organization that puts customers at the center, what we do when no one is telling us what to do is unlikely to be customer-centered behavior.

In speaking to people at every level in every kind of company—

those that have become thoroughly customer centered, those few that started out that way, those that are struggling with the change—we've found that the importance of culture is inescapable. How did employees naturally think about a problem before anyone told them how to think about it? What objectives immediately came to mind? What tools, what measures for gauging success? Which did the culture consider more important, simplifying the lives of managers or the lives of customers? Becoming truly customer centered means employees at every level immediately respond to these questions in customer-centered terms. It means they think naturally and in a sophisticated way about responding to customers' total needs, about treating different customers differently, and about creating economic profit.

When a company transforms itself from being organized around products, territories, or functions to being organized around customers, the shift in culture can be summarized as follows:

From	To
Products matter most.	Customer experiences matter most.
Internal efficiency leads to success.	Engaging customers leads to success.
Product data is key.	Customer data is key.
Employees want to be functional or product-innovation stars.	Employees want to be on teams that win with customers.
Customers are demanding and an annoyance.	We value making a difference in customer experience.
All customers are created equal.	High-profit and high-potential customers deserve a superior experience.

To test whether a company has overcome the obstacles to putting customers at the center, ask: Is it part of the culture? Do employees put customers at the center even when no one is telling them to do it?

Managing the Transition with All Constituencies

Because becoming truly customer centered is such a thorough transformation of a company, it affects every one of the company's constituencies: the board, investors, customers, employees. So the transition must be managed with each of them.

The board

A company-wide transformation is obviously a board-level issue. The wise manager would not think of making a change like this without board discussion and approval. Since the board's primary duty is to represent the interests of the shareholders, it's most appropriate to present the matter to them in terms of the stock and its performance. That means making the hair-on-fire argument outlined earlier, all about the life-or-death importance of economic profit and a premium P/E.

After establishing a sense of urgency, it's time to get into the principles of customer centricity and what it really means. This will involve outlining action plans on the technical, political, and cultural fronts. We can tell you from experience that it will be important to prepare for skeptical, quick responses. The problem is that people like to fit new ideas into the framework of what they already know. So you can be quite confident that someone will ask

> ⋎   Isn't this just a version of CRM (customer relationship management)—and aren't we already doing that? (No, it isn't just a version of CRM, and this isn't at all like anything we've been doing up till now.)

⅄ This sounds like another monster IT project—and omigod, the last one cost us zillions and got us nowhere! (This isn't an IT project, it's a comprehensive, company-wide strategy to create shareowner value by making managers accountable for customers; it involves IT, just as everything a company does nowadays will involve IT. It's the transformation of the company to create mutually beneficial value exchanges.)

⅄ Is this the latest marketing program? (No, it isn't a marketing program at all. It's a new and better way to organize and manage the company.)

We can also tell you from experience that by far the best way to get directors to appreciate the importance of being customer centric is to show them data about the company's most profitable and least profitable customers, on an economic profit basis, accompanied by an explanation of what those customers are doing for, or to, the company's P/E. Better yet, ask directors to volunteer their own guesses about who the company's best and worst customers are, perhaps with a guess about the magnitude of profits earned from each one. It is virtually guaranteed that these guesses will be dramatically wrong. When directors realize this, the discussion becomes very serious, very quickly. You've got their undivided attention.

Fortunately, it's possible to generate these profitability numbers without huge investments of money or time. Preliminary data derived from sampling (in companies with many customers) or customized analysis (in companies with few customers) can be produced in a short time, sometimes in a matter of weeks, and it is critical in setting the stage for the board's discussion of this transformation.

It's important for directors to understand that customer centricity creates an overwhelming competitive advantage. As we argued in Chapter 5, organization structure can and should be used as a powerful competitive weapon. The huge potential to drive the stock that comes from being customer centered is a real attention grabber. Then realizing that competitors lack this potential adds a whole new dimension to the discussion.

No matter how well directors understand the case for value proposition management and customer centricity, there's a strong chance they won't be willing to commit the entire company to it without running some kind of test. They are, after all, fiduciaries for the shareowners. They must be prudent. And running a pilot project is a perfectly valid step, presuming the entire timetable lasts months, not years.

Investors

At a time when most companies are desperate for positive attention from investors and analysts, becoming customer centered is a great story to tell Wall Street. It's new, it's different, the case for it is enormously powerful, and best of all, *it includes a direct line of sight to the stock price*. The central feature of customer centricity as we have described it is that customers drive a company's stock. A great company has to create mutually beneficial value exchanges between customers and shareholders. Thus, everything about customer centricity is connected directly to economic profitability and value creation; that is what managers are ultimately measuring and managing. This is, of course, the language Wall Street understands.

Customer centricity creates a competitive advantage not only in the customer markets but also in the capital markets. The reason is that customer-centered firms can give Wall Street valuable information about their operations that other companies cannot supply. The truth is that investors would love to screen their holdings on customer-based value creation analysis of the type we've described—but with the great majority of companies, they can't. On an income statement, much of any company's customer economics is buried in the line called SG&A (selling, general, and administrative) expenses.

Since that line also includes expenses like accounting, human resources, and legal, it's virtually useless for figuring customer economic profitability. The wide variation in how expenses are categorized means SG&A as a percentage of revenue can range from 85 percent for Yahoo to about 5 percent for Starbucks.

In the post-Enron environment many companies are publishing far more data than before, but they're still excluding key pieces of extraordinarily valuable information: customer acquisition costs, maintenance costs, length of customer relationships, and some sense of how customer economic profitability is distributed. The great majority don't even report how many customers they have, how many they gained in the past year, or how many they lost. A few companies—some wireless phone operators, credit card companies, cable TV companies—supply some of this data as it applies to the average customer; you may recall how we were able to use such published data to calculate some revealing figures for AT&T Wireless. But none we're aware of provides insight into profit distribution and how the company's actions are changing it. Yet knowing the distribution, for reasons we've discussed at length, is critical in deciding whether to buy the stock. Some managers may fear that revealing this information would supply competitors with powerful weapons. There's always that risk. But experience has persuaded us that the noncustomer-centered firm won't know what to do with this information, and indeed may very well misuse it. As long as most competitors are not truly customer centered, the risks of publishing customer profitability data are far less than the opportunities in using it to win investors. Bottom line, customer-centered firms can supply this information and show how they're using it to create value. Competitors can't.

Like directors, Wall Street analysts are paid to be skeptical; after all the nonsense companies have told them, that's understandable. So they, too, may want to see the results of a test or pilot. A company that wants to create the greatest possible impact on analysts might announce that it is, in effect, conducting a test without a safety net. It might tell the analysts, before the test begins, that it has identified certain segments of customers as high profit or high potential, has gained new insight into their needs, and has created innovative new value propositions that will be executed in certain identified stores with a particular group of customers for a given length of time, and the company will report the results. When the results support management's position, the positive effects will be dramatic.

Employees

In managing the transition with employees, the main issue is resistance. The transformation we're talking about is thorough-going, and while many employees may embrace it, they are the least of your worries. As with any major change, a number of employees can be expected to resist it. Why? In Professor Tichy's terms, resistance is of three types: technical, political, and cultural. Technical resistance is seemingly rational, based on logical arguments about costs, implementation, etc. Political resistance is based on whose ox is being gored; some managers will gain power, others will lose power, still others will get new bosses or subordinates and will be suspicious of what it all means. Cultural resistance is based on changes to the unspoken norms of behavior in the company, which don't change easily.

That's a lot of resistance. The essence of meeting it is that one does not respond to it piece by piece. Trying to do so would take all of management's time and would never succeed; putting out employee-resistance fires individually would be so laborious that new fires would pop up before the old ones were out. Corporate transformation is something the world has learned a lot about in the past twenty years, and one lesson is that top management replaces an old order with a new order. In the new order, there may be new leaders.

There will be new values, such as the company view dominating the silo view. There will be new criteria for hiring, developing, and evaluating people.

None of which means there will necessarily be mass firings. When it comes to employees, this process is first and foremost about evangelism from the CEO. Next the top leadership team has got to feel it owns the change and teaches the next layers of management about it. After that it's a matter of shining spotlights on best practices. The big idea throughout is showing employees at every level that this is how to win, and winning is fun.

During the transition, human resources processes must be finely attuned to whether employees understand the new order, and how they feel about it. Overt resistance is not necessarily a bad thing. The employee who speaks his mind, even critically, is someone who can be talked to rationally about the transformation, and who may point out legitimate problems. If it turns out he really isn't compatible with the new order, then everyone is better off if he puts that fact on the table. At a software company that decided to become customer-centered, a high-level executive walked into the CEO's office and said he thought the change was a terrible idea. "Customers are *stupid*," he said. "We can't possibly listen to them as we design our software." This executive ended up leaving the company in short order, which was clearly the best thing for him and for the company.

A greater danger than overt resisters by far, based on our experience with many corporate transformations, is passive resisters: employees who seem to go along, who mouth the words, but who quietly do everything they can to keep things the way they were. Rigorous HR processes are more important than ever at times like this. Evaluations should eventually identify such employees, who may have objections that can be worked out or who may need to leave the company for the good of everyone. There's a time to get tough, and this is it. Not living the new values, or maneuvering for personal power at the expense of shareowners, customers, and other employees are capital offenses.

Customers

The best advice for managing customers through a company's transition to customer centricity can be summed up as: Don't tell them what it might be, show them. This is the constituency that is already being managed throughout the transition. Since they are what the transition is all about, the effects *must* be apparent to them. In some cases their interaction with the company may change. A buyer for a large industrial customer may deal with a new executive at your company, for example. In cases like this, it's important to tell the customers what is changing and why—and most important what's in it for them. Some bad stuff may happen during the transition. But if the culture really changes, resolution of problems may be the most powerful way to persuade customers the company really has changed.

While we've talked about how executives can manage the transition to customer centricity with a company's constituencies, we foresee a day in the near future when the impetus to make this change may flow in the opposite direction. As the advantages won by the early movers become more apparent, the pressure to organize around customers will rapidly become irresistible. Boards of directors will begin demanding to know whether the current value exchange between a company and its customers is mutually beneficial. They will insist on seeing customer financial information as part of their own due diligence and will challenge management to act on it. Investors will demand that companies report it. They will have to because knowledge of customer finance will enable companies to attract investors away from companies that don't have this knowledge. Again, the advantage of raising capital on more attractive terms will far outweigh concerns about disclosing competitively sensitive information.

Once a customer-centered company has nailed down the practicalities of the organization transformation, and not before, it's ready to think about the role of mergers and acquisitions in creating and sustaining a premium P/E. The late nineties were the greatest merger wave in history, yet the great majority of those deals were massively misguided, resulting in at least $1 trillion of shareowner value destruction. But there is a better way, a way to turn mergers and acquisitions from a loser's game to a winner's game. It capitalizes on a customer-centered organization's core knowledge: which customers generate economic profits and which generate losses. M&A is scary and extremely dangerous terrain. That's our next topic.

△ 10 ▽

A Better Way to Do M&A

How to Stop Takeovers from Making Shareowners Poorer

Does this sound like a recipe for disaster? Your business is throwing off loads of cash each year, available to be invested. You've cut costs like crazy, maybe a bit too much; customer care and new product research are starting to suffer. Wall Street is demanding significant growth, but you know (and are trying not to admit) it just isn't in your strategic plan.

The disaster is what often happens next: a great big acquisition, which brings the buyer a desperately needed shot of growth. Trouble is, hard experience shows that 70 percent to 80 percent of acquisitions fail, meaning they create no wealth for the shareowners of the acquiring company and often destroy wealth. The problem is huge. Deal volume during the historic M&A wave of 1995 to 2000 totaled more than $12 trillion. By an extremely conservative estimate, these deals annihilated at least $1 trillion of shareowner wealth. For perspective, consider that the whole dot-com bubble probably cost investors $1 trillion at most. That's right: Stupid takeovers did more damage to investors than all the dot-coms combined. And while M&A activity has slowed, it hasn't stopped, and it never will. Unless practices change, misguided managers will keep right on making their shareowners poorer.

That's remarkable when you think about it. Many of these mergers have been done by the world's biggest, most successful companies, advised by elite Wall Street investment bankers who scored 1600 on their SATs and hold advanced degrees from Ivy League schools. Yet the great majority of these deals still lose money for acquiring shareowners (though they never lose money for the investment bankers— maybe they're not so dumb).

What's wrong? Do buyers have any hope of improving their odds? The answer is yes. Look at M&A in light of Principle One— that a company is a portfolio of customers—and it's clear why most deals are losers. Five key insights show how acquirers go wrong, and lead to a prescription for how companies can greatly reduce their odds of destroying shareowners' wealth through bad acquisitions. As we have argued, the key to realizing and sustaining a premium P/E is investing the operating cash flow a business generates in new business investment opportunities that will earn large returns in excess of capital costs for years into the future. For a truly customer-centered company, these opportunities will arise in various customer segment business units. Being organized around those units, and planning and managing the business on that basis, will probably cause managers to identify highly focused, specific merger and acquisition opportunities. In addition, being skilled at creating, communicating, and executing value propositions will be a key asset in making those deals value creators rather than value destroyers for shareowners.

▶**Insight No. 1:** To see if an acquisition will succeed or fail, look at the balance sheet, not just the income statement.

Imagine a company with the following financials:

	$ millions
Revenue	1,000
Costs	900
Net operating profit after tax	100
Invested capital	500
Return on invested capital	20%
Cost of capital	10%
Economic profit	50

Let's assume further that this is a growing company, and that Wall Street has rewarded it with a market value of $2 billion. The company has achieved this market value of $2 billion using only $500 million in capital; the difference, $1.5 billion, is the amount of shareowner value creation. So we could add to the above table:

Market value	2,000
Shareowner value creation	1,500

Now suppose you want to buy this company. Acquirers almost always have to pay a premium over the market value of a company, known as a control premium, since it's usually worth more to control a company than to own a small stake and just go along for the ride. A 50 percent premium is not out of line for an attractive target; for this company that would mean a price of $3 billion. If you buy it for that price and do nothing to change the operations of the company, look what happens to its financial performance on the books of the acquirer (changes in boldface):

	$ millions
Revenue	1,000
Costs	900
Net operating profit after tax	100
Invested capital	**3,000**
To pay market value	**2,000**
50% control premium	**1,000**
Return on invested capital	**3.3%**
Cost of capital	10%
Economic profit	**–200**
Market value	2,000
Shareowner value creation	**–1,000**

Notice that the operating characteristics of the business haven't changed. Revenues, costs, net operating profit after tax, and preacquisition invested capital are all the same; so is the cost of capital.[1] As a result, the intrinsic value of the business is the same, $2 billion.

(For simplicity we assume here intrinsic and market value are the same. If this were a publicly traded company that got bought by some larger company, its market value of course would no longer be observable in the stock market, but the business would still have an intrinsic value, and as long as the operating characteristics didn't change, this value wouldn't change either.) If profits were all you looked at, the deal could seem attractive. For an acquirer with profits of $300 million, this acquisition would increase profits by a huge 33 percent (that is, from $300 million pre-acquisition to $400 million post-acquisition, ignoring acquisition costs). Further, acquirers often claim they'll achieve cost synergies, increasing profits significantly. Suppose this buyer believed it could double the target's profits, to $200 million beyond any acquisition costs. That's the perspective from the income statement, and it looks great.

But now let's look also at the balance sheet, where the company keeps track of capital. The acquirer has invested $3 billion in the target company, so its $100-million profit represents a tiny 3.3 percent return on invested capital—a huge comedown from the pre-deal 20 percent return. Even if the profit-doubling synergies are fully achieved, which they rarely are, the return is still just 6.7 percent (a $200 million return on $3 billion of invested capital). Assuming investors are looking for at least a 10 percent return, this deal is destroying shareowner value for the owners of the acquiring company.

In its basic outlines this is a completely typical acquisition. So what is the acquiring company thinking? Since the deal looks like an obvious loser, how does the acquirer intend to make it a winner? First, the acquiring CEO is probably under tremendous pressure from Wall Street to reinvest cash and grow reported earnings, and may be hearing from investment bankers that if he or she doesn't make a deal, a competitor will; so merely completing an acquisition may be the CEO's definition of success. Second, many acquirers simply ignore the balance sheet effects. They don't care and maybe don't even know that they've whacked ROIC (Return on Invested Capital) down to a value-destroying level. Third, acquirers typically believe they can make a deal pay off in two ways, neither of which usually works well:

ⱴ   Cost savings. In most deals the acquirer claims it will save tons of money by combining functions. If two banks merge and each has a branch at a certain intersection, they'll close one. The two companies had two CFOs and now they need only one; ditto for most other staff positions. The merged company will be buying supplies, services, and raw materials in larger quantities and so may get larger discounts. If it works, cost cutting could certainly begin to solve the problem. But it usually doesn't work, in part because acquirers, caught up in the excitement of the deal, tend to be too optimistic about what's possible. In the example above, a 10 percent required return would mean profits would have to rise from $100 million to $300 million (10 percent of the new invested capital, $3 billion)—and it would take a brazen buyer to count on that much synergy. Significant cost savings have proven extremely difficult to achieve; in fact, integrating operations of two companies often *incurs* large incremental new costs as armies of workers focus on merging incompatible systems and cultures or on fighting turf battles.

Another reason cost savings rarely rescue mergers is that they can get bargained away in the negotiation of the selling price. The seller can usually estimate potential savings at least as well as the buyer, so he knows he can push for a price that conveys to him (and his shareowners) nearly all the value creation the cost savings would produce. Thus, once the deal gets done, achieving even all the hoped-for savings isn't enough to make it a winner.

ⱴ   Increasing revenue is the other way acquirers believe they can make high-priced mergers pay. Probably the most frequent claim for big deals is that they will create enormous opportunities for cross-selling. When Citicorp merged with Travelers, Citicorp was going to sell Travelers' insurance and brokerage service to its millions of customers, and Travelers was going to sell Citicorp's banking services to its customers. When AOL bought Time Warner, AOL was going to sell on-line advertising to Time Warner advertisers and vice versa, and Time Warner would sell AOL subscriptions in its magazines and deliver AOL over its cable TV systems. And so on with most of the big deals of recent years. The revenue of the combined company would be greater than the combined revenue of the two companies separately.

Cross-selling does happen, but almost never as much as the acquirer hopes. The problem is usually organizational. Tell an executive for Business A that he is now also selling the products of Business B, and the trouble starts. He doesn't know anything about Business B. He's afraid that if he sells Business B's products, his customer will spend less on Business A's products, which he knows how to sell. Another huge issue:

How does he get paid? Business B already has a sales force. Are they helping him? Why should he help them? And on it goes. Almost never is the acquirer or target organized around the customer, and after the transaction no one even thinks about it. It's too late, and everyone focuses inward, on integration. It's all the antithesis of a customer-centered company.

Result: The typical merger fails. In this case, an acquisition turned the target company from a big winner into a big loser. But you'd never know it if you considered only the income statement. When managers or investment bankers justify deals on the basis of earnings, earnings per share, or EBITDA—without addressing the balance sheet effects—watch out.

▶**Insight No. 2:** In most (though not all) mergers, the acquirer is buying customers.

Companies buy other companies for many reasons, but the most common is to acquire customers. Consider the ten biggest deals ever, as of spring 2003, all of which happened in the past few years:

↗AOL Time Warner

↗Pfizer-Warner Lambert

↗Exxon Mobil

↗Comcast-AT&T Broadband

↗Verizon-GTE

↗Travelers-Citicorp

↗SBC-Ameritech

↗Pfizer-Pharmacia

↗Nationsbank-BankAmerica

↗Vodafone-AirTouch

Go down the list and it's clear that most of these acquisitions were acquisitions of customers. This is true even when lots of physical assets are involved, as in SBC's acquisition of Ameritech. When one phone company buys another, or one financial services firm buys another, what's being bought and sold is ultimately customers.

While that isn't the only reason for deals, even the other reasons are customer related. Companies buy companies to get real estate or other facilities, to get brands, trademarks, patents, or technology, sometimes even to get employees. But all these common rationales are a bit imprecise. When a company buys another company to get anything other than customers, then it is buying capabilities to help it serve existing customers better and more profitably, or to help it acquire new customers. These can be entirely legitimate reasons for a deal. For example, when IBM buys a small, specialized software company, it likely isn't buying customers, since the target company's customers are probably IBM customers already. Rather it's buying new capabilities for serving existing customers better—or to put it another way, filling gaps in its customer value propositions.

Still, most deal volume represents companies buying and selling customers directly—and mostly not very well. As you look at the list above, do you notice anything? Those ten deals pretty well represent deals overall when it comes to performance: Most have been huge losers for shareowners. While the exact amount varies day by day, the aggregate loss of shareowner wealth since these ten deals were done is staggering—hundreds of billions of dollars.

▶**Insight No. 3:** In most companies, the distribution of customer profitability is much wider than managers suspect.

This is no surprise in light of our discussion of deaveraging. But most acquirers and sellers have never performed the docile analysis we've been stressing. Once the managers of an acquiring company understand that what they're really buying (directly or indirectly) is customers, they can take the next, far more revealing step in the analysis: understanding, as we have seen so often, that some customers are more profitable than others. With that observation in mind, and combining it with the fact that most takeovers are acquisitions of customers, it becomes possible to analyze deals in a new way.

Let's take another look at the typical deal described above, this time adding the reasonable assumption that the target company's customers can be classified into four quartiles of widely varying profitability.[2] From most profitable to least, we'll call them the Darlings, the Dependables, the Duds, and the Disasters. For simplicity we assume the company's capital is divided equally among the four quartiles, and we've assigned each one an after-tax operating profit; we won't take you through the whole spreadsheet behind the numbers in the tables below, but with this data we can calculate the shareowner value created by each customer quartile through a process we've described in earlier chapters.[3] For example, the Darlings quartile has an estimated intrinsic value of $3 billion, while $125 million of capital has been invested in it, so its shareholder value creation is $2.875 billion. Here are the numbers for all four quartiles, before the company is acquired:

	Darlings	Dependables	Duds	Disasters	Total
Revenue	250	250	250	250	1,000
Net operating profit after tax	113	63	13	−88	100
Invested capital	125	125	125	125	500
Return on invested capital	90%	50%	10%	−70%	20%
Capital cost	10%	10%	10%	10%	10%
Economic profit	100	50	0	−100	50
Intrinsic value	3,000	1,600	125	−2,725	2,000
Shareowner value creation	2,875	1,475	0	−2,850	1,500

The net result is the pre-acquisition $1.5 billion of shareowner value creation noted earlier. The Darlings (this company's angels) generate 200 percent of the economic profit and 192 percent of the shareowner value creation. The Disasters (its demons) are almost symmetrically disastrous.[4]

Let's assume this company is acquired on the same terms described previously. Because a great deal of new capital is added to the business, we've already seen how the buyer loses from this investment. Now we can see how this value destruction is divided among the customer quartiles. (Assuming the acquirer is not customer centered, it will not know pre-deal economic profit by quartiles and thus allocates the extra capital equally among them.)

	Darlings	Dependables	Duds	Disasters	Total
Revenue	250	250	250	250	1,000
Net operating profit after tax	113	63	13	–88	100
Invested capital	**750**	**750**	**750**	**750**	**3,000**
Return on invested capital	**15.1%**	**8.4%**	**1.7%**	**–11.7%**	**3.3%**
Capital cost	10%	10%	10%	10%	10%
Economic profit	**38**	**–12**	**–62**	**–163**	**–200**
Intrinsic value	3,000	1,600	125	–2,725	2,000
Shareowner value creation	**2,250**	**850**	**–625**	**–3,475**	**–1,000**

The most obvious fact leaping out of this table is that overpaying for the Disasters, the company's least profitable customers, is wrecking the whole deal.[5] Suppose it were possible to shut down and write off some of the assets being used for them, and to redeploy other assets and some costs to the other quartiles. As a result, many of the Disasters would no longer be customers, so the quartile's value destruction would be reduced, while the other quartiles would increase in value through the use of new assets. All the other numbers remain the same—but the totals change dramatically:

	Darlings	Dependables	Duds	Disasters	Total
Revenue	**300**	**270**	250	**50**	**870**
Net operating profit after tax	**160**	**90**	13	**0**	**263**
Invested capital	**850**	**800**	750	**100**	**2,500**
Return on invested capital	**18.8%**	**11.3%**	1.7%	**0%**	**10.5%**
Capital cost	10%	10%	10%	10%	10%
Economic profit	**75**	**10**	–62	**–10**	**13**
Intrinsic value	**4,500**	**2,010**	125	**–60**	**6,575**
Shareowner value creation	**3,650**	**1,210**	–625	**–160**	**4,075**

Note a few key points:

⅋ Shutting down some of the target's worst customers and redeploying some assets to other quartiles where they can be better utilized, the acquirer changes this deal from a big loser to a big winner. Shareowner value creation increases from minus $1 billion to $4.075 billion. Is it possible to shut down the apparent demon customers? As we discussed previously, a retailer can't stop people from walking into its stores but might be able to shut stores, make physical changes in its stores, or change marketing and customer service, in ways that would discourage chronically unprofitable customers; at the least it could stop pursuing and encouraging unprofitable customers, which many companies unwittingly do.

⅋ While jettisoning customers produces dramatic results in this example, there would probably be even better alternatives. Most companies can make unprofitable customers profitable. If an innovative acquirer could create new value propositions to serve Disasters, it might make some of them profitable. Recall Fidelity's efforts to migrate unprofitable customers to different delivery channels, lowering the cost of getting a stock quote from $13 (by calling a rep) to 1¢ (online). The resulting increase in shareowner value would be even greater than that shown above.

⅋ In the example above, a customer-centric acquirer made the deal a big winner—but a customer-centric target company could have been an even bigger winner without a deal. If the target company had eliminated Quartile 4 on its own, *before* the deal, shareowner value creation would have increased from $1.5 billion to nearly $6 billion (the new market value, $6.575 billion, minus the original invested capital, $500 million plus small investments in Darlings and Dependables), and most likely the company would never have become an acquisition target. In fact, such knockout performance would likely have earned the company an even higher market value than the one we postulated because investors would have awarded this better-managed company a new, higher P/E multiple, which would have discouraged even the most foolish prospective buyer.

▶**Insight No. 4:** Corporate acquirers are buying customers in bulk rather than one by one, so they should logically get a discount; instead they usually pay a premium.

When you go to the supermarket in the autumn, you see apples by the thousands. As you walk into the produce department you arrive first at big display cases loaded with brightly polished apples, from which you may choose the ones you want and put them in a plastic bag; they're $1.29 a pound. Nearby you'll usually find big brown paper bags already filled with apples. You can only see the ones on top, and you have to buy the whole bag; the price works out to 89¢ a pound. Depending on your needs, your finances, your mood, you decide which way you want to buy apples that day.

When a company buys another company in order to get its customers, it is buying customers in the big brown paper bag, and it usually can't even see the ones on top. If the target company is like most companies, it will have no customer financial analysis; no one will know which customers are economically profitable and which aren't, or the elements of customer profitability. Almost certainly no one will know how customer profitability is distributed.

Though the target company doesn't know these things—indeed, especially since it doesn't know them—it almost certainly has many unprofitable customers. But when an acquirer buys this company, it has to buy the whole bag, taking the bad ones with the good. Pricing, however, doesn't work the same as in the supermarket. Usually it's just the opposite. Customer financial analysis reveals this as one of the most remarkable and important facts about mergers and acquisitions.

Acquirers generally pay more than the market price of a target company's shares because they have to pay a control premium, described earlier. But this new analysis places the concept of the control premium in a new light. Control may indeed be worth paying extra for, but only in the context of a customer financial analysis that tells the acquirer what it's really getting and how much that seems to be worth. Without such an analysis, the acquirer may end up paying not 89¢ a pound or even $1.29 a pound, but $1.89 a pound for the apples in the big brown bag.

A customer-centered acquirer can be thought of as having X-ray vision—able to see through the paper bag. If it's loaded with bad apples, the company can avoid paying $1.89 a pound for an inferior collection of apples (or customers).

▶**Insight No. 5:** Buying profitable customers at premium prices can be far superior to buying a company.

This discussion leads to a larger question that's important for every company: In general, does it make more sense to acquire customers in bulk through acquisitions or one by one through marketing, opening new stores, and other means? The dynamics of M&A suggest an answer.

It all depends on price, of course—virtually any deal can be worthwhile if the price is low enough. The trouble is that in most acquisitions, especially if the target is a publicly traded company, more than one bidder is in the picture. Indeed, if the first bidder's offer is low, another bidder is almost certain to jump in. The problem for bidders who have analyzed the target's customer finances is that competing bidders often have not done this analysis and may therefore be willing to offer far higher prices. The customer-savvy bidder, who knows these prices are too high and cannot lead to a value-creating deal, is forced to drop out. He knows that to prevail he would have to pay $1.89 a pound for customers in bulk, and he also knows—a crucial point—that he has a much better alternative: paying $1.29 a pound for exactly the customers he wants.

If managers are surprised by the wide variation in customer profitability, they're positively shocked by the amounts they could afford to pay to acquire just the best customers of a target company. In our acquisition example, let's suppose the target company has a million customers divided equally among the Darlings, Dependables, Duds, and Disasters profitability quartiles—250,000 in each one. So the company's pre-acquisition market value of $2 billion works out to $2,000 per customer. The acquirer who pays $3 billion is thus paying $3,000 per customer, and as we've seen, this price makes the deal a big loser.

But suppose it were possible to buy just the best customers, the Darlings. In many businesses it may be possible to buy just some of the customers. In retailing it's possible to buy or open certain stores as a rough proxy for customer segments. In credit cards or certain other financial services businesses it may be possible to buy certain customers directly. Supposing an acquirer could buy just the Darlings in our example—how much would they be worth?

The answer, believe it or not, is that the deal would be shareowner value-neutral at a price of $4,500 per customer.[6] That is, if the acquirer could buy the Darlings for anything less than that price, the deal would create shareowner value. Of course a seller that hadn't analyzed customer profitability might be willing to sell these customers for much less.

But even if the seller wouldn't or couldn't sell just the best customers, this analysis shows that companies can afford to spend remarkably large amounts—in the form of marketing and other customer-acquisition costs—to get customers that match the criteria of the Darlings. (We're assuming the company, being customer centered, can deliver value propositions to retain the customers long enough to make the math work.) In this case, bringing in those customers at any price below $4,500 each would make the acquirer more valuable, and would be far superior to buying the whole company full of customers, even at the much lower price of $3,000 each. Managers across a range of industries often fail to appreciate just how much they could and should pay to win the most profitable customers—investors with over $10 million in investable assets, frequent fliers who pay full fare in first class, frequent repeat customers at hotels, restaurants, and casinos, for example.

There's evidence that successful companies understand this choice. Consider two groups of companies we've met before: the Dynamite Dozen, which all maintained P/E multiples consistently above the S&P 500 average multiple for five years, and the Dismal Dozen, whose multiples consistently trailed the average for five years.

Dynamite Dozen
- ADP
- Bed Bath & Beyond
- Dell Computer
- General Electric
- Home Depot
- Kohl's
- Medtronic
- Microsoft
- Pfizer
- Starbucks
- Walgreen
- Wal-Mart

Dismal Dozen
- American Express
- Bank of America
- Chubb

- ∀ Citigroup
- ∀ Delta Air Lines
- ∀ General Motors
- ∀ JP Morgan Chase
- ∀ Merrill Lynch
- ∀ Morgan Stanley
- ∀ SBC
- ∀ Sears
- ∀ Verizon

How do these groups compare with regard to M&A? The Dismal Dozen have been among the largest acquirers in America. Specifically, among these companies:

- ∀ Citigroup is the result of one of the largest mergers ever, between Citicorp and Travelers;
- ∀ General Motors bought Electronic Data Systems in one of the largest deals of its time, a huge and unproductive acquisition it later spun off;
- ∀ Morgan Stanley's merger with Dean Witter was one of the largest ever in its industry;
- ∀ SBC bought Ameritech in one of the biggest ever telecom mergers;
- ∀ Verizon is the product of multiple giant telecom deals involving Bell Atlantic, Nynex, and GTE.

By contrast, the Dynamite Dozen in general just don't do many deals, and the few they do tend to be small. Microsoft, for example, bought Great Plains Software, a small North Dakota company; Starbucks bought Seattle's Best Coffee, a small competitor. In general, though, these companies have grown organically, and at terrific rates. By far the biggest acquirer in the Dynamite Dozen is General Electric, which may make hundreds of acquisitions in a given year. But most of these deals are very small, rarely involving a competing bidder. As a result, GE can be highly disciplined about the prices it pays.

▶Prescription: Understand customer profitability—your own company's and that of any prospective target company—before trying to grow through M&A.

The reason most companies make acquisitions is to grow, often because the core business isn't growing enough, while the CEO is under pressure to reinvest cash from operations. But look again at these two lists of companies and forget for a moment that one comprises great performers and the other comprises poor ones. Just ask which group looks more like a list of hot growth companies. The obvious answer is the Dynamite Dozen—yet this is precisely the group that doesn't make many acquisitions.

The lesson is that it's possible to grow quite impressively without buying customers in bulk. More important, in order to grow in a way that creates shareowner value, it usually makes more sense to acquire customers *one at a time* and acquire *just the right ones*.

It's legitimate to ask whether the Dynamite Dozen have avoided acquisitions, and have achieved their success, by understanding the customer financial analysis we have outlined here. In the case of Dell, the answer is an emphatic yes. But for many of the others, the answer is that, like the great majority of companies, a number of them don't know customer profitability or other customer financial measures nearly as thoroughly as we advocate. But most of them do have a much better grasp of these factors than average companies do.

Why is that? The explanation is that seven of the Dynamite Dozen are retailers, while only one of the Dismal Dozen (Sears) is. Retailers, by the nature of their business, have a rough understanding of customer segment profitability because each store can be thought of as representing a customer segment, characterized by the traits of the customers who live around it. The experience of major retailers that have analyzed customer finances through sampling is that customer profitability often varies much less within stores than across stores. For the same reason, retailers can choose—again in a fairly gross way—the kinds of customers they add by choosing where to locate new stores. Excellent retailers regard different stores as individual customer segments with differing traits and needs; in response, these retailers stock each store differently in order to maximize profit. To repeat, they aren't exactly managing customer segment profitability, but they are approximating it by managing store profitability. By doing this they are able to fix, close, or sell unprofitable stores, which means they are making a reasonable first cut at eliminating the unprofitable customers that sap value from so many companies.

Acquisitions aren't necessarily a bad idea. If buying another company can bring an acquirer profitable customers, or can help it create a better value proposition or better execute its current value proposition, then it can make sense. As more companies become truly customer centered, we can expect to see deals based on value proposition management skills. When a potential target company possesses such a capability, it can be worth a substantial premium to a buyer who understands it, since it enables the acquiring company to create ever better value propositions that generate ever more economic profit.

It becomes a question of whether the acquirer has a sophisticated understanding of customer finance. The type of value analysis described in this book and especially in this chapter will certainly help managers decide what they ought to ask for and look at in due diligence and then pay in an acquisition. As that analysis shows, in practice it isn't easy to make a deal at a price that lets the acquirer create value.

M&A, like other aspects of running a company, works best when seen as a way to create shareowner value through customers. Whether such a view, universally adopted, would result in more or fewer deals is impossible to say. Value-destroying deals of the type we've seen so often wouldn't happen, but acquirers with an advanced understanding of customer finance might see acquisition opportunities that no one had seen before. The one thing we know for sure is that if executives saw M&A in this new way, shareowners would be a lot better off.

By now we hope we've motivated you to take the next steps in your company toward becoming truly customer-centered. No doubt you're wondering what you can do about it on Monday morning. That's what we take up next.

△ 11 ▽

Your Action Plan

What to Do on Monday Morning

How do you get started?

We've described an integrated approach to transforming a company from a traditional organization centered on products, territories, or functions into one that's truly centered on customers, and we've shown how this change enables a company to reward shareowners with a rising stock price and a premium P/E. It's a big, multidimensional change for any enterprise. Each of the elements we've described plays a critical role. But for the change to be as effective as possible, most of these elements—and preferably all of them—need to be implemented as a holistic, integrated system.

While each company's journey through this transformation will be unique, the starting points will be similar. The questions asked, the first steps taken—these are things we can identify with confidence for any company. If you're serious about driving your share price by putting customers at the center, here's how to get started. Through the following steps, you can lay out an action plan for transforming your company.

Where Are You Now?

Review your company's results on the quiz at the end of Chapter 1. Specifically:

a. Identify your primary areas of strength and weakness, the items on which you got the highest and lower scores.

b. Verify your view with key colleagues by handing them the quiz and comparing results. In companies where we've conducted this exercise we have often found wide disparities among different managers' opinions. For example, members of the top team often don't agree on a description of the company's current value proposition. In many cases they can't even articulate it. These differences need to be identified and talked through before the company can make progress toward the transformation.

c. Identify which of the problem areas are primarily educational deficiencies and which are the result of cultural, technical, or political obstacles. For example, it may be that your company has not established a premium P/E as a corporate goal but could enthusiastically pursue that goal once the logic for it is understood. This is an educational deficiency that can be readily corrected. On the other hand, your company may have a deep cultural belief that all customers should be treated the same; or it may follow a longtime practice, reflected in how managers get paid and promoted, that revenue growth is what counts; or it may have a history in which no one but a successful territory manager ever got to the top. These are much bigger obstacles. All of them need to be identified.

d. Based for now on intuition and experience, prioritize the opportunities you see for becoming or remaining a premium P/E company. That is, of the seven items described in the quiz, which offer your company the greatest potential for driving the stock price, and which offer the least?

e. Identify the specific steps you can take to raise your company's score into the 50- to 70-point range. Only a tiny fraction of companies are in that range now. Getting your company there can create large opportunities for competitive advantage.

Understand Why Your Relative P/E Multiple Is What It Is and Identify Key Opportunities for Improvement and Competitive Risks

a. Does your company have a premium P/E, an average P/E, or subpar P/E multiple? *Don't* compare your company's multiple with the average for a group of industry peers; remember that in the race for investors' capital, you're competing with all possible investments. So compare your multiple with the average for the S&P 500—the figure is published in the *Wall Street Journal* every Monday. Then compare your company with the average multiple quarter by quarter over the past five years. (For quarters in which your earnings are distorted by big onetime losses or gains resulting from write-offs or asset sales, for example, you'll want to normalize earnings to get a meaningful P/E.) Over the past five years have you been premium, average, or subpar?

b. Determine the nongrowth value of your company's current operations, which is equal to its net operating profit after tax divided by its cost of capital. For example, if a company has a net operating profit after tax of $5 million, and its capital cost is 10 percent, then the value of its current operations is $50 million. After determining this current operations value for your company, compare it with the company's total market value. If the total market value is larger, then the difference reflects the value of future growth the market is counting on you to achieve. If the total market value is smaller, then the market is expecting your company to destroy value.

c. Calculate or estimate your company's values for the four factors that determine P/E: return on invested capital, cost of capital, investment, and duration.

d. Compare your company's values with the values that characterize the premium P/E sweet spot:

Premium P/E Sweet Spot

- ∨ return on invested capital > 25%
- ∨ capital cost < 12%
- ∨ investment (in excess of depreciation) > 70% of earnings
- ∨ spread duration > ten years

Where are you falling short? Which gaps are the largest?

e. Compare the market's implicit expectation of your future growth with the reality of your company's values for the four factors (see note 4 in Chapter 4). Is the market expecting your company to invest more than your internal evaluation suggests is possible? Is the market failing to give you credit for growth prospects that you believe are healthy? Or is the market's evaluation of your future growth pretty accurate—for better or worse?

f. Determine how much the four factors would have to change in order to create a price that would give your company a premium P/E. If you are already a premium P/E company, determine where you may be most at risk from your most threatening existing or potential competitor.

Begin to Calculate the Economic Profitability of Your Customers

a. Figure the true economic profitability of your products and services, being sure to allocate all operating costs and capital, and to do it appropriately.

b. Then observe, perhaps through sampling, the product and service bundles purchased by customers and calculate the profitability or unprofitability of the various baskets.

c. Then calculate, again through sampling if necessary, the customer-specific prices, discounts, costs, and capital (such as accounts receivable) of various customers.

d. Combining all of this data, and again making sure all the company's costs and capital (including goodwill) have been included, make a first pass at calculating the economic profitability of customers.

e. Categorize your customers into deciles by economic profitability.

Assess Your Company's Needs to Reorganize Around the Customer

a. Determine which organizational structure currently matches that of your business.

b. Determine which customer-centered organizational structure would best enable your company to serve customers better and achieve the levels of the value elements required to reach or sustain a premium P/E.

c. Describe the accountabilities you would establish in your new structure. Who, specifically, would be accountable for profit and loss? Would this accountability be shared? If so, would the incentive effects be diluted by sharing? Would the new accountabilities incentivize managers to maximize total shareowner value creation from customers?

d. Contrast the desired accountabilities with the current state. Who, specifically, would gain organizational power? Who would lose it?

Segment Your Company's Customers in a Way That Holds the Greatest Potential to Create a Sustained Premium P/E

a. Identify the common characteristics of customers in the top decile of economic profitability and of those in the bottom decile. Determine *why* the top and bottom decile customers are where they are. What specific elements make them so extremely profitable or unprofitable?

b. In addition, analyze your customers based on their behavior, such as propensity to use certain channels or to buy certain bundles of products, or other behaviors that are important in your business.

c. Incorporating the learning from the customer profitability and behavioral analyses, overlay an analysis of customer needs, met and unmet, and their relative importance. Determine candidate segments based on customer needs. This is not a completely scientific or precise process. Apply the Segmentation Matrix to help your analysis as you subsegment and regroup, searching for sets of segments to go with. In any case, this is always an iterative process. Companies continually revisit and refine their segment definitions.

d. Divide each needs-based segment into profitability deciles. Incorporate the behavioral analysis, consider subsegments.

e. Complete a Customer Segment Value Creation Scorecard for each segment based on its current value proposition.

f. Using the economic profit and intrinsic P/E multiples for each segment as calculated on the Scorecard, determine which customer segments are currently helping or hurting the company in its quest to achieve or maintain a premium P/E.

Begin Developing a Practical Value Proposition Management Capability

a. Begin synthesizing your current customer segment knowledge. What are each segment's needs, profitability, behavior, attitudes, and demographics? Where are the holes in your knowledge? How will you fill them?

b. What is your current value proposition for each customer segment? How does it compare with competitors' in meeting the segment's needs?

c. Using customer data and insights, hypothesize improved value propositions for each customer segment. Specify how they would improve the segment's Value Creation Scorecard. Focus on key operational drivers, such as churn, close rates, or new customer acquisitions.

d. Test and verify each hypothesis with concrete experiments. Set up careful controls to guard against exogenous factors' rendering experiments useless. Identify winning value propositions.

e. Determine a plan for communicating each winning value proposition.

f. Before executing, rerun your scorecard, reestimating the expected economic profit of each customer segment to see if the new approach will accomplish its goal: increasing the value of a given segment enough so that it moves the company toward a premium P/E. If not, then reformulate the value proposition or the plans for executing or communicating it. Create new experiments if necessary.

g. Form plans for communicating and executing winning value propositions in a big way.

h. Track learning from the experiments and scaling, continually updating the customer segment knowledge inventory.

Plan How to Organize Around Customers

a. Outline in detail the new, customer-centered organizational structure you intend to adopt.

b. Identify the technical, political, and cultural barriers in your organization that will have to be overcome. Develop a plan, with specific accountabilities, for overcoming each type of obstacle.

c. Describe your plan for selling the reorganization to your board. Can you write a script for the CEO to use?

d. Describe the communication plan you will use with your company's senior leadership team.

e. Describe the communication plan you will use with your broad workforce.

f. Outline your pitch to investors to get them on board.

g. Describe exactly what you will say to customers about the change. Will the message be different for different segments? Will it differ on the basis of customer profitability? Is a message even necessary for some customers?

Make M&A a Winner's Game

a. Is a merger or acquisition essential to the success of your corporate transformation?

b. If your answer is yes, explain why you can't meet your desired goals by acquiring customers one at a time, through sales and marketing strategies, or in small groups, for example by acquiring retail stores.

c. If you still feel a merger or acquisition is essential, describe your due diligence plan for assessing your target and the price you will be willing to pay. How will you understand the economic profitability of the target company's customers, and especially the distribution of customer profitability? Explain how you will analyze the balance sheet effects of the deal to insure it does not reduce your company's economic profitability.

Develop Your Time Line

a. Create a chart displaying the component tasks along with how these tasks depend on one another, of the key elements of your plan, including significant milestones—who, what, when.

b. Ensure that this process will be *fully* completed in two years or less. If it cannot be completed in that time, organizational fatigue will almost certainly kill it before the benefits are realized.

c. Describe all the other initiatives you will drop in order to make customer-centric transformation the only leadership priority. If you don't do this, your organization will not believe your determination, and the tremendous technical, political, and cultural barriers to creating a truly great customer-centric business will defeat you.

It's time for action. Right now, someone in your industry is beginning to understand how customers are the ultimate source of shareowner value. That company's managers will figure out who their most profitable and least profitable customers are. They'll find ways to delight the best customers and get more of their business, and they'll find ways to make unprofitable customers profitable—or let them go, to become unprofitable customers of some company that can't tell the difference. They'll make sure every customer is "owned" by a specific manager, and they'll show managers how to know if they're creating or destroying shareowner value. Then they'll hold managers accountable for creating tons of it. When they acquire new customers, they'll know what they're getting and how much to pay. They'll leave competitors to overpay for whole companies in value-annihilating acquisitions. Because they understand the connection between their only source of life, customers, and their ultimate bottom line, shareowner value, they'll create value by the truckload.

Which company in your industry is doing all this? That may be the most important question you face in your business life today—for whether you will be victim or victor depends on it.

Notes

Chapter 1: The Trillion-Dollar Opportunity You're Missing

1. Return on equity (ROE) is simply a company's profit divided by its share-owners' equity (assets minus liabilities). ROE is the most widely used performance measure for financial institutions like this bank.

2. Return on capital is net operating profit after tax, divided by invested capital. We'll expand on this concept, and how it's figured at the customer level, in later chapters.

3. See Chapter 5 for a discussion of Wal-Mart in this regard.

4. American Express, Bank of America, Chubb, Citigroup, Delta Air Lines, General Motors, JP Morgan Chase, Merrill Lynch, Morgan Stanley Dean Witter, SBC Communications, Sears Roebuck, Verizon Communications.

5. Source: Nicholas Heymann, Prudential Securities.

Chapter 2: Will This Customer Sink Your Stock?

1. This is actually total enterprise value: the market value of all outstanding shares plus the market value of the company's debt.

2. While impressive, this figure is lower than it was the previous year because investors got worried about potential problems with the credit risks in the company's portfolio of customers. All these figures were calculated by the Stern Stewart & Co. consulting firm.

3. For simplicity, we've ignored the fact that Capital One's share price reflects not just the value of its current customers, but also the value of additional customers that investors expect the company to add later—that is, net new customers, in excess of those who defect. Ignoring those future customers for the moment is a

simplification worth making because it gets us started down the path of conceptualizing the value of a customer.

4. This average customer value is emphatically not the same as a customer's LTV (lifetime value), a concept that has been much discussed in recent years. As typically calculated, LTV doesn't account for the critically important capital used in a business or for all the company's actual costs. The full extent of its deficiency will have to wait until we discuss the elements of the P/E ratio, which should be the basis of a company's financial goals.

5. As with Capital One, we're simplifying this example by ignoring the portion of value that investors have assigned the company based on expected future growth (though in this case it's legitimate to wonder if investors expected any future growth).

6. Managers often ask us, "Shouldn't this be incremental analysis?" That is, shouldn't we just look at how much incremental capital is associated with a given customer? The answer is no, as we explain in Chapter 3.

7. Since we made some adjustments to reported capital in the previous step, we'd have to make sure we took account of these by making adjustments to reported net operating profit after tax.

8. To be completely rigorous, you would want to assign different capital costs to different customers, based on the expected volatility of the future economic profit from each one—the greater the expected volatility, the higher the capital cost.

9. This $1.536 billion is the total enterprise value—the total market value of the company's equity and debt, the same figure we looked at when considering Capital One and AT&T Wireless. To keep the Multimax example simple, we'll assume the company has no debt. So $1.536 billion is simply the market value of the company's stock.

Chapter 3: The Astonishing Truth About Customer Profitability

1. Though traditional accounting rules require the $1,000 acquisition cost to be treated as an expense, a management accounting perspective would argue that for internal purposes it should be treated as capital investment and ammortized over the expected three-year duration of the customer.

2. That is, ($250 million + $150 million) / $250 million

3. "Do You Know Who Your Most Profitable Customers Are?" *Business Week*, September 14, 1998.

Chapter 4: Managing Customer Profitability the Right Way

1. As is standard, total return to shareowners is defined as percent price appreciation plus percent yield on dividends.

2. For example, suppose your company had a P/E of 25 when the S&P 500's P/E was 25, then you would be on the 100 percent line. If your P/E was 12.5, you would be on the 50 percent line.

3. In the recent economic slowdown, several companies, such as Coca-Cola and Procter & Gamble, have lowered their financial targets. That may be perfectly appropriate as the environment changes, but the goal of beating the market's P/E remains appropriate no matter what. Just lowering expectations in absolute terms and not committing at least to beating the merely average company will hardly inspire confidence in management.

4. The premium P/E sweet spot numbers should be thought of as rules of thumb based on capital market conditions in early 2003. The formulas underpinning these calculations go back more than forty years to a classic paper by Nobel laureates Merton Miller and Franco Modigliani, "Dividend Policy, Growth, and the Valuation of Shares," *The Journal of Business* (October 1961). Making a number of simplifying assumptions, a company's enterprise value, V, can be expressed as

$$V = \frac{Nopat}{CC} + \frac{Investment * (ROIC - CC) * D}{CC}$$

where Nopat is steady state net operating profit after tax, CC is capital cost, Investment is the amount invested annually in the future in the business, ROIC is return on invested capital, and D is duration. From this expression it is easy to compute a company's P/E. For further discussion there are several useful references. One classic academic source is T. Copeland and J.F. Weston, *Financial Theory and Corporate Policy*, Third Edition (Addison-Wesley Publishing Co., 1988). Another excellent source is by Martin Leibowitz, former vice chairman of Salomon Brothers and current vice chairman of TIAA-CREF: M. Leibowitz and S. Kogelman, *Franchise Value and the Price/Earnings Ratio* (Research Foundation of the Institute of Chartered Financial Analysts, 1994). Michael Mauboussin, managing director and chief U.S. investment strategist at Credit Suisse First Boston, has written a number of pieces on inferring market expectations about duration and spread from current share prices. For example, see M. Mauboussin, "Competitive Advantage Period (CAP)," Credit Suisse First Boston Research Report (October 4, 2001).

For management it is usually easy to estimate the level of future investments, return on invested capital, and capital costs. To get a feel for estimating duration, it is generally very helpful to use the formula cited above, but in reverse. That is, instead of trying to estimate enterprise value, V, start with the actual enterprise value at a point in time based on a company's market capitalization and debt, and then make assumptions about all the other variables and solve for duration, D. This is the starting point.

5. It's becoming increasingly common for a single company to bring in revenue from all three sources. For example, General Electric has applied this principle in its medical equipment and power systems businesses, among others. The medical equipment business sells machines like CAT scanners to hospitals; the power equipment operation sells giant generating turbines to electric utilities. Those are products with good but not spectacular returns on invested capital. Both businesses have found, however, that customers will happily pay for services that help their machines run more efficiently, even if they're not broken. In some cases the company may go much further: If a customer is expanding into Asia, for example, GE may offer its expertise from having operated there for years. The returns on these services are much higher than on products. GE also offers software that helps optimize the operations of a customer that uses its equipment. The returns here are much higher still.

6. Though invested capital can be a bit more complex because it needs to reflect the credit risk of the products and the customers buying them.

7. More specifically, the company's intrinsic P/E is determined by the four factors: return on invested capital, capital cost, investment, and duration. Each of these factors is a weighted average of the customer segments' four factors.

Chapter 5: Organizing Around Customers

1. After a highly successful tenure at Fidelity, McGovern has since retired to teach at the Harvard Business School.

2. Jay Galbraith in *Designing Organizations* (Jossey-Bass/John Wiley & Sons, 2002) provides an excellent discussion of the organizational design issues involved in organizing around customers, as well as other structures. He discusses how the choice of design can be viewed as a powerful competitive weapon.

3. Wal-Mart's Sam's Club business, a chain of membership warehouse clubs, possesses data on all customers since each must present a membership card in

order to buy merchandise. But the company apparently doesn't use the data in the customer-centered ways we talk about.

4. Jay Galbraith, "Building Organizations Around the Global Customer," *Ivey Business Journal* (September 1, 2001).

Chapter 7: Knowing and Winning Customers

1. An excellent discussion of the concept of value propositions and their characterization as a complete experience is provided by Michael J. Lanning in *Delivering Profitable Value* (Cambridge: Perseus Books, 1998).

2. The subtlety here is that the precise financial effect will depend on the business's ratio of fixed costs to variable costs. If the business has high fixed costs (these are typically industrial businesses), then losing a single customer may yield only a slight decline in total costs; in that case the company needs to replace the lost unprofitable customer with a profitable one. In a company with high variable costs (such as the service and information businesses that account for most of the U.S. economy), simply losing an unprofitable customer may increase the company's economic profit.

Chapter 8: Driving It to the Ledger

1. Two of those four initiatives, six-sigma quality and digitization, can be hugely valuable to an organization becoming customer-centered. The six-sigma discipline, with its emphasis on process mapping, helps a company understand exactly how it delivers its value propositions to customers, an understanding that is surprisingly hazy at many companies. Digitization, GE's term for applying information and Internet technology to create shareowner value, can be an invaluable tool for becoming customer-centered at big organizations.

Chapter 9: Becoming Truly Customer Centered

1. N. Tichy and S. Sherman, *Control Your Destiny or Someone Else Will* (New York, Harper Business, 2001). See especially the section, "The Handbook for Revolutionaries."

Chapter 10: A Better Way to Do M&A

1. For simplicity we're ignoring some technical nuances (involving issues such as taxes and amortization) that one might argue change some values in the table.

2. For purposes of this analysis we're talking about strict profitability quartiles, not the needs-based customer segments described in Chapter 6.

3. In these tables, the row labeled Market Value needs a bit of explanation. The value shown for the company as a whole is literally the market value as observed in the market. The values shown for the component customer profitability quartiles cannot be observed in the market, so they might be better thought of as the previously mentioned "intrinsic value." In this example we again make the simplifying assumption that intrinsic value equals market value.

4. Conceptually it may seem a bit difficult to think of a customer quartile, such as the Disasters, generating negative market value. After all, you've never seen a stock that sold for a negative dollar amount. Nonetheless, the Disasters deserve their negative value because of their financial characteristics, which, if not fixed, will certainly drain value from the company. Indeed, the illusion of averages will preclude management from seeing that this quartile will be reducing net operating profit after tax by $88 million a year and more than likely growing until something is done.

5. Suppose after acquiring the company management discovers the true intrinsic value of each quartile. Reallocating more of the acquisition capital to the Darlings and Dependables would not by itself remedy the $1 billion of shareowner value destruction. The acquirer paid six times invested capital for the whole company ($3 billion for a company with pre-deal capital of $500 million). The pre-acquisition intrinsic value of the Darlings is about twenty-four times capital, so paying six times the original invested capital would still have resulted in positive economic profit and shareowner value creation. The problem is that paying six times invested capital for the Duds and Disasters is a disaster. That massive overpayment has to come out of the "skins" of the Darlings and Dependables, but it can't. That's the issue.

6. Thus the total investment for 250,000 customers would be $1.125 billion, and capital cost at 10 percent would just equal the Darlings' net operating profit after tax. A confident customer-centered investor could pay up to $12,000 per customer, based on the intrinsic value of $3 billion.

Index